Spiritual Communication with Families on the Other Side

with ISABELLA JOHNSON
TRANSFORMATIVE MEDIUMSHIP

COMPILED AND EDITED BY

NANCY L. BILBAO, M. A.

ISBN 979-8-9986877-0-9 - eBook
ISBN 979-8-9986877-1-6 - Paperback
ISBN 979-8-9986877-2-3 - Hardcover

Book Layout: Chrissy Hobbs, Indie Publishing Group Inc.
Cover Design: Britt Wilson, Indie Publishing Group Inc.
Copy Editing: Mary Metcalfe, M.S., Indie Publishing Group Inc.

This book is dedicated to everyone who has ever shared their loved ones in Spirit with me. A huge thank you to Nancy Bilbao–you're an incredible gift to the world and I am a better person for knowing you. To my family, you're my inspiration for what I do. To my daughter Courtney, who I know I will see again one day–Mama loves you.

Isabella Johnson

CONTENTS

PREFACE BY

ISABELLA JOHNSON

My intention with this book is to provide evidence that relationships and bonds with those we love continue after physical death and to give hope to those struggling with grief or loss.

I have always seen dead people. As a child and young person, it could be very frightening to open my eyes from sleep or turn a corner in the house and encounter someone unexpectedly. I cannot imagine a day without this gift some forty years later!

I am honestly not sure of how my gift works. I know those on the other side show up in my consciousness, seeking to connect with their loved ones who remain on earth, and I can act as a conduit between them. Those in Spirit and I merge thoughts, memories, and emotions, and I can relay their life events as if I am recalling them. I feel their feelings in those moments of life—joy, sadness, disappointment, pride, and so on. I simply try my best to deliver their messages, thoughts, and emotions to my clients.

I am unsure if they merge with me or me with them. This process remains somewhat of a mystery to me. In combining with those in Spirit, I initially experience their physical death. I've been comforted learning that physical death is brief, with detachment, and also without pain or lingering effects. Compared to birth, it is a much more natural process. We are going home, back to a welcoming embrace.

Those in Spirit continue by sharing what was learned in this life. Regrets are often mentioned of a highly personal nature, acknowledging ways in which they could have done better in personal relationships.

Mediumship can be a truly transformative experience, and I am humbled and honored to play a small role in that process. This process is therapeutic. Questions are often answered, and there is a genuine desire to provide a resolution on the part of those in Spirit. Your loved ones do all the work, and although I am a poor substitute for them, I try to honor them by relaying their thoughts and words as compassionately and accurately as possible.

Their highest priority is to let each of us know that after death, we all continue and that their love and connection to us never dies. I hope the personal accounts shared here provide you comfort and wish to thank those who shared their journey for their vulnerability, honesty, and healing in this journey.

I struggle to share personal details of my life because I genuinely do not feel it is relevant to the bigger picture of my work: providing evidence of life after life. I am a daughter, sister, wife, and mom. I have been blessed to love and be loved so deeply, and at this juncture of life, I can also understand the blessing of knowing loss on a grand scale. Had I not experienced loss, I do not think I would be prepared to empathize with or bring healing to my clients.

By far, the most challenging loss was that of my daughter. Initially, I found myself in the depths of despair, and there were many days I did not want to live. I was unsure how to survive experiencing such a deep and profound pain.

Even with my work as a medium, I questioned everything about the afterlife. It took years for me to process and find solace in my grief. On a very human level, I still believe no parent should ever bury a child. It feels wholly unnatural and almost perverse.

As the days turned into months and years, finally now, decades later, I more deeply understand this profound experience as an opportunity to become more gnostic, to search for personal meaning and understanding of what God/Source is and the sense of our existence here. Although that period was the hardest of my life, I can now express gratitude for the gifts it delivered, but please know it did not come quickly or easily for me. I lost every bit of faith I possessed. I felt emotions I did not fathom could exist. I lost relationships, and even myself, in this journey.

What has emerged from the ashes is an absolute knowing that our souls are eternal, that in Spirit, we still possess individual traits and deeply understand the purpose and meaning of our lives. Everything but our souls is transitory, *EVERYTHING, everything.* After rebuilding our lives, what remains here on earth is something so sturdy and strong—indomitable even–knowing that we will see our loved ones again and find meaning in the remaining days.

Today, I have no dogma in my life, and what I believed before my child transitioned now feels like child's play. I am no longer afraid to ask questions and continue searching for a clearer understanding of life. My path to understanding continues to evolve day by day.

Some days are hard, and I lapse back into grief because it has been such a constant companion. Other days, try as I might, I struggle to recall how I could ever be so bereft, so distant that it feels that the experience occurred to someone else, totally disassociated from my being. On other days, I have moments of profound feelings of separateness from the Source, and on different days, I feel ecstatic, intermingled with all that was or ever will be.

In other words, my journey has looked very similar to yours.

Isabella Johnson
Arkansas
March 2025

PART ONE

HEALING JOURNEYS

WALKING HAND-IN-HAND

ISABELLA JOHNSON

Losing a child is the most difficult event in one's life. It rips your soul into a million pieces. Breathing seems almost impossible. We feel as if we have lost everything, and, in a way, there is truth in that. Initially, it can be hard to find a reason even to live.

We ask ourselves, "Where are they? Do they know how much we love them? Will we see them again? Are they with us still?"

These and thousands of other questions flood our minds and souls in a desperate waterfall of panic. As a mother who has walked this path, I am so grateful when our children provide irrefutable evidence that they still exist and are with us every second of every day. They know our thoughts and emotions and want to comfort us in our grief.

I meet the best people—my clients and their loved ones in Spirit.

The following story tells the reflections of a client whose child gave us such proof—not only of how our love does not die but also of how they walk with us daily.

ERIC AND CYNTHIA BUTHER

"Santiago is encouraging us, cheering for us, and telling us how proud he is of us from the other side."

Eric: We've been married for twenty years. Santiago, our oldest, was born in 2010 in Charlotte, North Carolina. Our daughter, Arianna, was born shortly thereafter. When they were in preschool, we moved to Lancaster, South Carolina. We wanted to live in a close-knit community.

Santiago was diagnosed with terminal brain cancer, DIPG (Diffuse Intrinsic Pontine Glioma), in 2018. We learned that it is inoperable and currently has no cure. The doctors told us our only course of action would be to find a clinical trial and start radiation treatments.

Santiago Buther

That started the whirlwind of our lives. We ended up at St. Jude Children's Research Hospital in Memphis, Tennessee. Initially, the treatment started to work. He did amazingly, but unfortunately, like most cancers, they come back a little stronger than they started. Then, we transferred over to Cincinnati Children's Hospital Medical Center. Unfortunately, the cancer again stabilized for a little bit, then it just escalated, and he passed on January 17, 2020. In our minds, it feels like it was yesterday, and sometimes it feels like it was forever ago.

Arianna was seven, and Santiago was nine when he passed. During the pandemic, I didn't really want to be around people, so it specifically allowed me time to grieve on my own and be in my safe space versus having to try to navigate being with people.

Cynthia: Two houses down from us is another family that had moved in two years previously. They had two teenage kids, a boy and a girl. The boy unknowingly rode his bike over a steep hill and into a tree that was in the woods near our house and passed away. When Santiago passed, I needed to talk to another mother who understood what I was going through. My friend mentioned the group Helping Parents Heal and Isabella Johnson. I considered contacting Isabella, but I was very skeptical about mediums possibly taking advantage of people, and I didn't want to have a bad experience because I was hurting so much. I didn't want anybody to take me for granted or anything like that, so it took me awhile before I reached out to Isabella.

I actually asked a friend to set up an appointment for me under her name. She even paid for it because I wanted a totally clean slate and didn't want Isabella to know my name or anything about me.

I didn't want to give her a chance to google our names and find out what had happened. So, when we talked to Isabella, we found out immediately that she was so kind, and her tone of voice was so friendly. She took it in stride when I revealed that I wasn't actually the person who had made an appointment and assured me it didn't matter. She explained how her process works, and made us feel comfortable.

Eric: Santiago didn't come through right away. Isabella described our grandparents, who came through first and then brought Santiago forward. We're Latino and come from a place that accepts mediumship and an afterlife beyond what some are typically used to seeing. I felt comfortable enough to have these conversations with Isabella.

The way she described my grandmother was so precise it made hairs stand up on my arms. Isabella picked up the fact that something was wrong with Santiago's head. Then she went into all the things that I was worried about concerning the decisions I'd made and our thought processes when Santiago was going through treatment. We had worried about the decisions we'd made along the way.

When things had been up against the wall, including dealing with clinical trials, we were unsure of what action to take or not to take. We had always had that doubt. Before we could tell her anything, Isabella described everything we'd done, line-by-line. Actually, Santiago was describing all of this to us through Isabella.

Isabella related that Santiago had acknowledged every little decision we'd made and how it impacted him. Santiago assured us that we had made the right decisions along the way.

Isabella also described our relationship, making everything more concrete. She described the layout of our house to a tee. She was viewing our house through his eyes, essentially. She relayed to us that Santiago's spirit is so strong. She said she was surprised that we hadn't felt or seen him at first because he's so connected to his family and home.

Arianna, Cynthia, Eric and Santiago at St. Jude's Children's Research Hospital in 2018.

We have spoken to Isabella several times. During one of our meetings, Santiago said, "*Daddy, you've got to cut the grass.*" It needed cutting, as I hadn't cut it in three weeks. We all laughed. There he was, calling me out! We were just shocked.

Another time, Santiago said he

liked the truck I had just bought and that I hadn't even told Cynthia about it yet. In fact, I hadn't told a soul until maybe an hour before our talk with Isabella. Santiago snitched me because it was a ridiculous, huge monster truck! We had wanted something to have fun in. I had told him, "Hey, when we beat this, we're going to get a Jeep. We're going to take the top down. We're going to try to take the mud!"

One of the ways I grieved was spending an hour, just as I had with Santiago when he was here in the physical, doing something together, like building Legos. I bought a Lego fire truck that had lights and a siren for Christmas the year he passed. I had just finished it when Isabella called, and she said that Eric wanted me to know that he loved the fire truck. Knowing this was so helpful to me.

I don't want to say that I was going to do self-harm, but I had a profound depression. Isabella showed how concerned she was about our family and relayed a message from Santiago. He said, "*Daddy, your thinking is not right. I need you to get better*!" Isabella had no idea I'd been building Legos before the reading in which she described it. She knew exactly what I was thinking to the last word.

Cynthia: Isabella can relay even the emotions we are all feeling. Santiago made it known that he loves his family; that he will always be with us; and that he is watching over us. Once, Arianna even saw him standing at the top of the stairwell. It scared her, and she ran into her room. Another time, during a reading, Santiago said he had fixed the lava lamp in his sister's room. He adjusted it so that only the color red was coming through. Red plays a big part in our life. It was almost like he purposely made it stay red so that we all knew that was his way of saying, *"Hi, I'm still here!"*

He's also letting us know that he's getting better in the sense that he's learning how to communicate with us or leave more signs with us. Isabella had said she's not surprised that we can feel him all the time or see him now because the connection between all of us is so strong.

For example, Isabella asked, "Can you feel his hand, because he shows me he is holding your hand when you walk?"

Eric: I did have another friend who lost a child two days after childbirth, and I immediately encouraged her to call Isabella. She was feeling similar to how I was feeling, experiencing so much grief. Her husband also mirrored my feelings. Being that the child was only two days old when it passed, it was so difficult. You're built up for the joy of childbirth, and then all of a sudden knocked down at the same time.

Their experience was very similar to ours. The mother needed to get to the point where she could say, "OK, I can breathe today."

Santiago's Support in Setting Up a Foundation in His Name

Eric: It really helps every time I talk with Isabella. Her validation was so helpful when we started a foundation in our son's name.

Sometimes, we just didn't know if it was the right thing to do. We were concerned about reentering grief all over again, dealing with terminal children. Sure enough, Isabella knew of our concerns before we even vocalized them, and not only did she validate what our reality is, she encouraged us, saying that not only are we doing the right thing on this side, but that Santiago is encouraging us, cheering for us, and telling us how proud he is of us from the other side.

We have many goals around our foundation for next year, our fourth year. It's called "Santiago Strong Foundation."

(https://www.santiagostrong.org).

We have been able to support parents whose children have passed. Santiago even called out one girl by the name of Esther, who had passed the night before. As crushing as it was, he helped her transition during that time because she was so young she needed not to feel fear at that moment.

This again validated what we're doing here on this side of the plane and that he is a part of it. It's not Santiago's sitting in his corner and doing his own thing. He is all on board and wants to help other kids in this situation. That's exactly his personality type, exactly what he would have done if he was here, and we all decided to do it together. It is so amazing. Again, a name like Esther you would rarely hear. It really hits home that the time we're spending here is value-added.

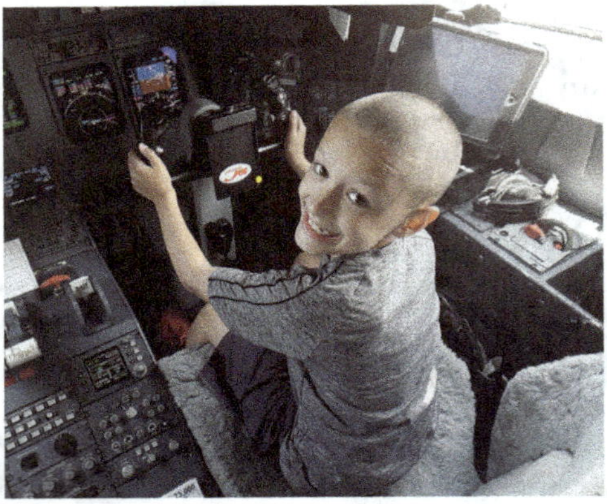

Santiago on a flight back from Saint Jude's Children's Research Hospital in Memphis, Tennessee. The staff saw the St. Jude's gear and asked if Santiago would like to see the cockpit.

Even when we were walking around Saint Jude, Santiago encouraged the other kids. He would say, "Let's play!" Some of those kids hadn't heard the word "play" since they'd entered the hospital. The parents were sometimes shocked to see Santiago embracing their children as he had. He was always doing something with the little kids that meant the world for them. This was his personality then and continues to this day.

This is why I'm not shocked that he's actively a part of our current family dynamics, including helping others.

Soulmates

Cynthia: Eric and Santiago look like identical twins. Their mannerisms are the same, and they finish each other's sentences. When you think of soulmates, you might think of a man and a woman, but in the case of Eric and Santiago, they are soulmates.

Isabella did bring that up. She said that Santiago and Eric are truly soulmates. That's why she was cautious about bringing up the fact that they continually live these lives together, and their purpose is to fight. She said that in a previous life, Eric and Santiago were brothers, and they died together in a war. Their purpose is to fight again in this life, but it is a different type of war. During a reading with Isabella, Santiago wanted to convey to Eric that they are fighters together in this life, which is a different type of fighting.

Eric: When Isabella talked about it, it was so chilling because she described him to a tee: his personality, the way he would have spoken to us, his energy. Because of Isabella's gift, we feel we are talking directly to Santiago. It is something that we needed, and we continue to need.

Sometimes, people have an issue with their religious beliefs and don't trust mediums. I understand that because there are mediums who take advantage of people. This is definitely *not* the case with Isabella. She is a kind, compassionate, authentic, and a totally accurate medium.

If I didn't have grief counseling, our family, and Isabella, I don't know where I would have been. Some people tell those who are grieving to "let it go," like it will get better on its own time. I've never felt those things. There is no reason to let him go because he's here. Having him here and knowing he's here means the world to me, and that's how I keep going. I don't have to say, "I have to get better." I don't have to say, "Let it go," because he's here. I'm never going to "Let it go" because I shouldn't have to.

Cynthia: Isabella reaches out to us on his birthday, which is a heavy day. She gives us an update on how he's doing. She's a very busy person. As a counselor, she has guided us through so much. She was kind enough even to let us know the process of our readings in detail, asking if we were comfortable, and so on. The way she speaks to us makes us feel like she knows what we are doing and why we feel this way. She helped us so that what we were about to hear wasn't a huge smack in the face, which could have made us feel. She stops midway through our reading to ask if we're all right.

We love spending a short time with her these days, hearing Santiago's name and knowing that she's there and we can contact her if we need to. We've emailed her several times following our sessions for clarification or trying to make sense of what we may have heard from Santiago.

Eric: Some are afraid, but having this information confirms and solidifies everything I have believed in my entire life. I know this is where we belong, and this is exactly what heaven should be. It's just so powerful.

I'm not lost. They're not lost. I don't even like using the words, "I lost my son." I did not lose my son. I know where he is. He is just not physically in front of me. So, I try to be careful with my words, too.

I want to share the knowledge and validation I've received from our readings with people next to me so that they can understand how powerful it is to have this information in your back pocket. It does solidify one's faith. Most faiths believe in the other side. This explains what heaven is.

A LIFE WELL LIVED

ISABELLA JOHNSON

I meet the best people in my work. The living are always hurting but hopeful, and those in Spirit *always* have a story to tell. I remember meeting Nolan a few years ago during a reading and trust me, he is a hoot! Opinionated, funny, kind—yet a man with little tolerance for laziness or foolishness. He loved his family more than himself and ensured they knew that daily. I am so grateful his family wanted to share their experience with all of us. May we all live as fully as they are.

I do not look for names or dates when I give a reading. I like the deep stuff, as I want to know their personalities, the details of personal relationships, and memories only my clients will know of. These are the ways I provide evidence.

Often, those in Spirit speak of regrets they might have, things left unsaid, or ways they hurt us and deeply regret. I intend for a session to provide deep healing and reconnection, validating life *and* relationships that continue. Nolan is a perfect example of this, and I can't wait for you to read his story!

We will always miss those we no longer see, but rest assured, they are only a breath away.

VIRGINIA STONE

"Good news. Bad news. I'll be by to pick you up in 20 years."

I want to introduce you to my partner, Ripley, my boxer. Looking back, we can see how things line up, and it is wild. We had another boxer, Ruby, who was my heart. She was fine, started panting, and three hours later, she was gone. I was devastated. Then, we got Ripley. It was about a year before Nolan passed.

Nolan, my husband, died on June 2, 2022. Later on, I told my daughter, Katy, "I know why Ruby died when she did. It gave me time to get Ripley, which helped me so much with Nolan's passing."

Typically, Nolan and I walked Ripley every day. We had a path that we went to that rounded through the woods and near a creek. It was nice and totally shaded. I didn't go the day he passed because I had a hair appointment. Sitting

Nolan Stone

Virginia and Nolan Stone

at home, I thought, *"He's been gone too long."* So, I tried calling him, but he didn't answer his phone. He had my car, and I got into his truck. When I got to the park, I saw my car still sitting there and knew something terrible had happened. I could hear Ripley barking.

Nolan had almost made it back to the car. I started running and found him. He was lying face down. They said he had just dropped dead. He had his left arm under him with the leash and his other arm lying back with palm up. I could imagine how he had been walking. It was entirely out of the blue. He had high cholesterol and diabetes, but they were under control with medication. He had even had a heart test done a year before he died, and it was okay.

I called my daughter, Natalie, to come down, and she called her sister, Katy. Natalie didn't know what to say, so she said, "Daddy's gone." Katy said, "What do you mean?" Natalie said, "He's dead, Katy."

I'm lucky enough to live next to my daughter, Natalie, who has me over for dinner every night. Katy is my financial advisor now and helps with keeping my bills in order. Nolan has made sure they took over his duties now that he is gone.

Nolan and I were married for fifty-one and a half years. He moved across the street from me when I was in fourth grade, and he was in fifth. We were always friends. We didn't start dating until we were in high school. When we got engaged, my mother-in-law told me that I was the one she had always wanted to be with her son.

Three Generations Meet with Nolan During Reading

We had a service about a week after his passing, but we weren't ready to say goodbye. I was sitting at Natalie's one night, and she mentioned her boss, who had met Isabella at a work event, and was blown away by her. I asked Natalie if she'd thought about meeting with Isabella, and she said she had. So, we arranged for a meeting with her. We were all hurting so freakin' bad. My daughters and two granddaughters were also there for the meeting with Isabella. We were in three different locations at the Zoom meeting.

As I said earlier, Nolan died on June 2nd, 2022. The first time we met with Isabella was on November 17th, 2022. At the beginning of this first reading, many people from the other side appeared, including my mom, dad, and Nolan. At first, we thought Nolan was someone else, but then he said, "*Tell them I'm not deaf anymore.*" He couldn't hear for nothing when he was here in the physical. He wasn't completely deaf, but he was very hard of hearing.

There was also a young man, 18-22-ish, who stood beside my daddy. This was before Nolan entered the conversation because when Nolan got on, he dominated it! Isabella said, "The grandkids or the kids don't know him, right?" I told her that she was right.

My daughter said, "Mama, it's Willie!" I thought it might be. Willie was the boy I dated in high school before Nolan, and he drowned right after graduating. Isabella asked if he'd been gone a long time. He said he had been gone for over fifty years, so we knew it was him. Isabella asked me if Nolan didn't like Willie at first. It wasn't that Nolan didn't like him, but he knew I would have married Willie if he had lived. Mama said Nolan always had his eye on me, even when we were friends. Daddy did not want Nolan to take me away, but there was no way to make a living in that little bitty town. Nolan was a bit of a rebel, but Daddy grew to love him. Willie told us he had been a guardian angel all these years, looking over everything.

Once we knew Nolan was there, we could confirm with Isabella that he was the one we were there to see. As the reading progressed, it felt like we were talking directly to Nolan. I had just gotten my hair done. My hairdresser had been asking me to stop bleaching my hair because of the damage it was causing. She had asked me just to dye it and go from there. I had finally given in that day.

Then Isabella asked, "Did you just have a hair appointment? Did you change your hair?" I almost fell out of my chair! I am a hair person. I am the kind of person who feels happy when my hair turns out right and unhappy when it doesn't. Nolan made a point to tell me he likes it, even from the other side. Every time we talk to Nolan through Isabella, he says he likes my hair. He knows how important it is to me and tells me about it.

Also, during the first reading, Isabella asked if anyone had recently lost a female. My eldest granddaughter, Madelyn, had a close friend who had recently passed away. Madelyn is twenty now. This happened when the girls were eighteen or nineteen. Her friend told Madelyn she heard her talking to her on the other side and appreciated her friendship. Isabella asked if there was a marker where she died. Madelyn held up her wrist and showed her a tattoo with the girl's name on it and the date of her death, which lends credence to how strongly we believe that she is talking to those who have passed. This is so amazing. There's no way that Isabella's a fake.

At this point, Isabella asked how long Nolan had been gone because he was butting in again, and we said, "Five months." Isabella said, "If I had known that, I would have asked my assistant to push you out a little further." She said people in Spirit will show up but sometimes don't share much information that soon after their passing. In Nolan's case, Isabella shared a lot of information with us, which, as Isabella mentioned, is unusual when someone has recently passed over to the other side.

Let me describe Nolan. He was eighty percent sweetheart but was also obstinate and had a short temper. Occasionally, he would go off on you when you weren't expecting it but he was a good person the rest of the time. The balance was worth it. During another reading with Isabella, he apologized and said he should have been more patient. He also let us know he's reading the Bible now, which is funny because he was agnostic here. It was fun saying, "I told you so!" to him. Now that he's on the other side, Nolan always gives us signs. He blinks the lights in the house like crazy.

We decided to meet with Isabella again about six months later. As soon as she saw us, she said she was hoping it was us when she saw Natalie's name on the schedule because she had so much fun the last time talking with Nolan. She asked if Nolan was a big rodeo fan because she had gone to a rodeo, and he showed up there with her! We told her he was a rodeo volunteer in Houston for over twenty years.

During these readings, Nolan always told me how much he loved me. At the second reading, he said, "*She is the cutest thing I'm ever going to see.*" Then Isabella said to herself after receiving a message from Nolan, "I'm not going to say that." Finally, she agreed and relayed that he had said, "*You're still the cutest little thing in the South, and you have the cutest rear end.*"

He always thanked us for giving him such a good life in our readings and said he didn't think he deserved it. That's something else he always said when he was physically here.

Messages for Children and Grandchildren

He told my girls, Natalie and Katy, how proud he was of them. Katy is an electrical engineer working on the Orion project at NASA. She is so smart. She graduated ninth out of her class of over 400 in high school. She never realized what an accomplishment that was, but Nolan helped her realize how smart she is.

My other daughter, Natalie, was a salutatorian. She got a Master's degree in History and tried law school but didn't like it. She is now a senior director of sales operations. They are both brilliant.

These girls and my sons-in-law are taking care of me. Nolan and I had talked about that before he passed. When Natalie and Katy moved closer to me, he said he was happy to have them so close because we were getting older.

Back row: Roger Moye, Katy Moye, Ginger Stone, Natalie Prescott, Eric Prescott
Front row left to right: Charlotte, Maddie, Nolan Stone

Our eldest granddaughter, Madelyn, is a Future Farmers of America (FFA) member and wants to raise goats and be a park ranger. During a reading, Nolan asked, "*Have you given Madelyn the truck yet*?" I hadn't yet told Madelyn that I was going to give her his truck. He spilled the beans! Nolan also told Madelyn that she would graduate from college and be what she wanted to be, which made us ecstatic. She tried very hard to get into Texas A&M and finally made it. Nolan was sure to make a point in the reading to tell her how proud he was of her accomplishment.

Nolan and Madelyn also shared a love of sports. One year after he passed, the Astros won the World Series. As an aside, I have kept his phone service on, and one day, I heard Madelyn leaving a message: "They did it, Pawpaw. The Astros won the World Series. I wish you could have seen it!" That's one of the sweetest things I've ever heard in my entire life.

Nolan and Virginia with their grandchildren, Maddie and Charlotte Moye.

I introduced my younger granddaughter, Charlotte, to Isabella as Baby Charlotte. She's eighteen and has had some difficulties due to a medical misdiagnosis in fifth grade. Once the doctors discovered what the underlying problem was, narcolepsy, about three years ago, she's made great progress and is blossoming now.

Charlotte has a great attitude and is level-headed. When Nolan talked to Charlotte during one of the readings, he told her to stop thinking she wasn't special. "*She can't see it. I want her to learn to see it*," he said. He also relayed that she would graduate from college and be what she wanted.

Charlotte has a vocabulary that won't quit. She writes poetry and edited college students' papers on the Internet when she was twelve. She was working on a poem for me, and I didn't know anything about it until we talked with Isabella during a reading. Nolan asked if she'd given the poem to me yet. He again spilled the beans on that one! I was born in the year of the Dragon, and she titled the poem "Moogie the Dragon." This poem is very symbolic. It's such an amazing poem.

Out of all of us, Charlotte's having the hardest time dealing with Nolan's death.

Isabella related how close Charlotte and Nolan were when he was with us. They would play computer games. Nolan was good at it. Her friends were blown away by how good he did. He was a good Pawpaw. The gaming sealed the deal. He would get a drink in the kitchen and head to his room, saying he had to contact Charlotte about a Wolf game they were playing. They were so close, and it was so devastating for Charlotte when he died.

In another reading, Isabella mentioned a lady talking about Thanksgiving and marshmallows. I then realized it was Aunt Dot, who always made a dish during Thanksgiving that we called the "green stuff." Aunt Dot said it wasn't marshmallows, and it was cottage cheese. When Isabella relayed Aunt Dot's message about "green stuff," Charlotte was pretty surprised, I'd say. If Charlotte had had doubts about Isabella and her Pawpaw being present in the readings, she knew then that Isabella was the real deal after that reading.

Nolan has my dog, Ruby, with him on the other side. Isabella mentioned during a reading that she didn't know why it was so important, but Nolan said it was essential to him that Isabella tell me that he has all the dogs. Billy Graham said, "If it's heaven for you, your dog will be there." Nolan knew that I wanted my dog there with him.

Siblings Heal Old Wounds

The second time we saw Isabella, my daughter asked about my sister, Earnie, at the end of the reading when Isabella asked if we had any questions. Katy said, "My aunt died recently, and I wonder if she has anything to say." Isabella asked, "Is she rigid? Did she go to church and that?" We said, "Yeah." Nolan rolled his eyes and said, *"Look over there."* Earnie's husband had died and was there, telling Earnie that she needed to apologize and make things right. She apologized, but it was half-hearted, like, "Ahh, I'm sorry."

My sister Earnie and I had had a falling out before she passed. She accused me of something I didn't do. A few years later, she wrote me a letter and apologized. And we had gotten back together. And then, life happened, and we weren't speaking anymore, and I didn't think it was my fault. My family didn't think it was my fault. She was jumping on me again, like the last time.

The next time we met with Isabella, Earnie came through initially. Nolan was there, and he rolled his eyes again. My sister honestly and sincerely apologized to me for the way she behaved. She said she was sorry to the point that Nolan said, "OK. That's good. All right." He said that was enough; we were all there to talk to him, not her. We laughed pretty hard at that, but it was true!

My other sister, Virgie, has dementia, and they're testing her for Alzheimer's. She's been sick. So, when talking with Isabella, I asked, "Could we know anything about that?" Isabella said, "We'll see." Then she said, "Nolan likes this one, doesn't he?" He does! He loves Virgie!

Another time, during a reading, Isabella asked, "Who is sitting in a chair?" We had purchased a loveseat instead of two individual recliners because Nolan said he wanted to be able to touch me. Nolan was left-handed, and I am right-handed. I started sitting on the left side after he died because that's where he used to sit. He said he loves who is sitting on the left side. I said, "Oh my God, it's me! It's me!"

Isabella asked, "Who's got the necklace?" I have a necklace I made in remembrance of Nolan after he died.

All of this makes me feel elated. The readings helped me, and they helped my daughters and my granddaughters. You would be on a spiritual high for a couple of days after meeting with Isabella. The things she tells us are so specific we know it can't be anyone but him!

I tell people we have a very close family. And we assumed, all four of us, that this is what every family is like until we're out and around other people. We had supper and a party almost every night. We would laugh. I was talking and laughing, and I would lose my breath. We had such a good life. Nolan said that to me just before he died. We were sitting on the couch, and he said, "You know, we had a lot of fun." And we have. We've had a lot of fun. I miss the hell out of him. He was a bear of a man. He was only five-foot-eleven tall. He told people that, and they'd say, "Oh no. He's got to be six-foot-six." Nolan had such a huge presence with us before he died, and it has continued on the other side.

When we first talked with Nolan during our first reading, he told me I'd live another forty years more. I was seventy. I'm seventy-one now. He was insistent. And the next time he talked to me during a reading with Isabella, he said, "*Good news. Bad news. I'll be by to pick you up in twenty years.*" Now I believe it. I have no fear of death. The only reason I wouldn't want to die now is because my daughters and granddaughters would miss me. I have to hang in there for a while. If anything were to happen to me right now, I don't think they could take it.

Isabella knows so much! We've now seen Isabella a total of three times. The things that Isabella would relate are always spot on. You couldn't ask for anything better than Isabella!

Nolan and I were married for fifty-one and a half years.

SUDDENLY YOU ARE GONE

ISABELLA JOHNSON

Life is full of the unexpected. It is as certain as the sun rises each day; we will have our lives disrupted by sudden events. When we lose a loved one unexpectedly, it can feel as though the very ground under our feet is no longer sturdy. There are no moments for goodbyes, to say "I love you," or "I am sorry."

At these moments, unraveling the reality that our loved one has transitioned to the other side, everything in life suddenly stops. We ask ourselves, "How are we still breathing?" or "How is it I must wake up and go to sleep without you in my life?" or "How do I get questions answered?" or "Am I doing things correctly?"

A billion emotions arise, most of which we were unaware existed. "Will we die from this pain?" or "How can I still be here?" I remember looking at my children as they slept and thinking I could not possibly survive if anything happened to them. I was sure my attention and love would keep them here long after I was no longer here. Then, the unthinkable happened, and I found myself still breathing after my child was not here. I had done everything right, or so I thought.

Rebuilding is hard, even excruciating. For those of us whose child has transitioned before us, we ask ourselves, "Who are we now that our loved one is gone?" Initially, success is measured by our ability to breathe, bathe, eat, and sleep. Our mind, once a perfectly formed complete puzzle, has exploded, and a piece or two will never be recovered. We spend months, sometimes years, trying to put the pieces back together again. We rework and rearrange our lives until a story reveals itself, providing us with a modicum of peace.

Then, more questions arise, and we find ourselves rearranging our thoughts. Days go by, then weeks turn into months, both dragging us along, flowing through the abyss of grief.

I remember after my daughter transitioned, I had no accurate gauge of time. When the first anniversary of her passing came, it felt as though it had been a million years, and at the same time, just hours since she had been with me. I needed to understand. I needed all of this nightmare to make sense.

Eventually, I had peace, but joy and purpose took longer.

When I am with a client who has had a child who has transitioned, I am mindful of our shared grief. In conjunction with those in Spirit, I attempt to provide those answers and help put the pieces back together again. An astounding young man in Spirit told me, "*We are not lost; you are. You feel lost without us.*" I try to incorporate his message when dealing with not only my own pain but my clients' as well.

Here is that young man's story. Meet Teo.

CECILIE SURASKY AND CAROLYN HUNT

"Teo has a message for you. He insisted I get through to you. His message is, 'Tomorrow is a new day!'"

A cheerful, loving, and kind young man, Teo had begun to experience anxiety during the pandemic quarantine of his senior year when he was also facing decisions about his future. Cecilie said, "I think at that time, he was also experimenting with transcendence. We'd spoken hours before his transition, and he told me he was really happy, which makes me think he wanted to extend that feeling."

This fatal accident devastated Teo's moms, friends, extended family, and larger Berkeley and LGBTQ communities. It launched deep processes of grief, spiritual expansion, and collective healing with the dozens of loved ones shocked, confused, and traumatized by his passing.

Cecilie and Carolyn received support from their loving extended community. They also reached out to Helping Parents Heal, a support group for parents who have lost their children.

In one of their first significant synchronicities, Cecilie had experienced her first session with Isabella several months before Teo's passing to connect with her father (who had passed at the beginning of the pandemic quarantine). At this second session, Isabella disclosed her personal experience with losing a child and her shock and sadness at hearing of Teo's passing. Isabella immediately became a trusted, skilled, and loving guide for their grief and healing journey.

Isabella quickly developed a clear connection and close personal relationship with Teo. She conveyed validated information, specific messages, humor, and other clear indicators of Teo's unique personality that served to accelerate the healing process, provide deep comfort, and facilitate the continuation of close relationships as the moms labored to adapt to this "new normal." In response to Teo's requests, she offered gratis sessions to Teo's other family members and friends in acute need.

The following is Cecilie and Carolyn's story of continuing and expanding their close, intimate, loving relationship with their son. With the guidance of healers—especially Isabella—their skills at recognizing and interpreting signs and synchronicities increase their telepathic communication abilities, study afterlife research, and share everything they're learning within their community.

In turn, members of their community have their own remarkable encounters with Teo, weaving a tapestry of love and connection.

Cecilie and Carolyn: We are married, live in Berkeley, CA, and are mothers to our beloved, joyful, and devoted son in Spirit, Teo. Teo transitioned suddenly and accidentally in July of 2020 at age eighteen, a month after graduating from Berkeley High School, by taking a pill provided by another young person that they both thought was Percocet but, tragically, contained Fentanyl.

Cecilie: One of the many things that made Teo's upbringing so unique was how he belonged to a large extended family that included many chosen aunties, uncles, and cousins. From the moment he arrived, he was raised in a circle of adoring love, and everyone stayed fiercely close. A beloved member of this circle who was particularly devoted to helping raise Teo was his Uncle Franco, who passed away suddenly in 2014.

Even after he slipped into a coma, Franco began sending text messages—proof to us that he was reaching out from somewhere in between worlds. After we made the painful decision to take him off life support, those messages continued, and Teo grew up with a constant awareness that Uncle Franco was around. We'd often casually ask, "What's Uncle Franco doing now?"

Carolyn Hunt, Grandma Hunt,
Teo Surasky, Cecilie Surasky

So, when Teo made his transition, it felt natural that Uncle Franco would be there to welcome him and that they would reach out together from the other side. Their communications and the countless 'impossible' synchronicities, which often left us gobsmacked, reminded us they were always with us.

Finding Isabella at the moment we needed her was one of those synchronicities. I had been listening to interviews with many mediums, but when I heard a podcast with Isabella, I sensed she was the right one for our family. At the time, my father had recently passed away, and I'd turned to Isabella to help me navigate my grief. When Teo passed just a few months later, Carolyn and I both met with her and discovered she too was a "Shining Light Parent," meaning she knew, in her bones, the grief of losing a child. She met us in our trauma and heartbreak in a way that, frankly, very few could.

In those first weeks after Teo's transition, we gathered with his friends—daily at first, then weekly, then monthly. Having lost Franco, I knew that losing a close brother can be just as devastating and that these kids needed help as much as we did. So, we went through the process of grief together. This means it was love that connected them to Teo, love that brought us together, and love in all its forms, which we allowed to flow in our home and within relationships.

Three-and-a-half years later, many of them have gone to college or graduated, but we are forever family now. Carolyn still texts with them regularly, and they visit whenever they're back in town. And they are largely thriving.

In the beginning, we couldn't see any possible way forward. It was a grief so large that it felt impossible to hold. I can only describe it as an experience of annihilation. But it was a paradox—the absolute worst experience became an initiation. This was partly because it was also the catalyst for waves of almost oceanic expressions of love—from and among our friends, family, Teo, Franco, Teo's friends, colleagues, and so many more.

Carolyn: First, I can say that Isabella is full of love and magic. The timing of our meeting with her was lifesaving. Many layers of emotional processing and meaning building evolved through our ongoing conversations. To tell a coherent story of our journey over the past three and a half years with her in words is challenging. I always pictured Isabella's readings as the spine, the backbone of our grief journey, with muscles and arteries created with other forms of healing and experience. We have an ongoing relationship with our son and many opportunities to connect with him through our readings with Isabella. Cecilie and I have read many books about metaphysics and mediumship. I think there's such a need for holistic, well-crafted portrayals of this process that I'm honored to be part of this one.

While Teo was with us physically, we had such a beautiful, happy life as a family of three in Berkeley. We had many crazy, fun times, enjoying each stage of his life and being very involved in his, including baseball and other sports, which he loved. His friends were always his high priority, and he cared deeply for them (and continues to do so). I can only describe the experience as one in which we were a strong, happy family going through some challenging times together during the pandemic, and the next second, everything shattered.

Even though Teo started talking to us immediately, I feel I was in shock for three years and am just now coming out of it. There's a lot that I don't remember; however, I do remember that when Teo first transitioned, the days were filled with people—people coming over, people bringing food, people bringing flowers.

Teo's high school graduation

Teo's friends were around constantly and were equally traumatized. To this day, we're closely involved with his friends, who've become family, which is a blessing. I'm now grateful for the peaceful way that our son transitioned. This is the first time I've been able to say that. To be honest, I'm going through a type of trauma therapy (EMDR or Eye Movement Desensitization and Reprocessing) right now that was strongly recommended and is helping.

This journey feels to me like a slow climb up many mountains. Isabella has helped us simultaneously go through grief and spiritual expansion.

Cecilie: I'd like to share a story about the origins of this tattoo on my arm. Just seconds after we took Uncle Franco off life support, Teo, who was eleven or twelve at the time, asked me for my phone. There had already been some fascinating, impossible cell phone activity from Franco, but we were not prepared for this. Teo took one look, handed the phone back to me, and asked, "'Mommy, what is this?"

It was the most extraordinary message that had simply appeared as a draft text: Following my three initials and the precise date of the last, joy-filled day I'd spent with Franco, there were three smiling faces, each with a different flourish unique to each of us (Teo, Carolyn, and me); a perfect ellipsis; and a fourth smiling face, Franco. It followed Franco's smiling face with a dollar sign and an exclamation point: :-D $! There were so many unique symbols in this message that it took toggling back and forth between four separate menus on my phone—two of which I didn't know existed—to complete.

Uncle Franco was saying, "I made it. I'm just an ellipsis away from you, and where am I now? Jackpot!" It suddenly made sense that if you embark on a journey, you first want to let your loved ones know you made it safely and that the view is beautiful! Teo was the first one who saw the message. Franco was making sure we knew he was right here, just a breath away, and now I wear it as a tattoo on my arm to remind myself that we're all together, even if some of us are in this dense, earthly form and some of us are in Spirit.

When we found Teo, we were annihilated—I don't want to understate the trauma and horror of that moment, and part of me disassociated to survive it—but I also think our souls knew he was alright. We knew because we'd already gone through this extraordinary opening up of portals with Uncle Franco. At my very first medium reading years earlier, when Franco, who was gay, teased the medium in a way she didn't quite comprehend but which was so true to him, I thought, *Holy smokes, this dude is alive. He's alive, and he has the same unique sense of humor. This is not a joke.* In that instant, I could feel my whole body change. I knew with my entire being that spiritual death was not real.

That realization came at an unspeakably painful price, but the loss of Franco was also what helped save us. Without Isabella and this community of people who openly communicate with their children in Spirit, I'm not sure how we would have survived. They showed us, again and again, that no bond of love is ever truly broken.

Multimodal, Multi-dimensional Communication

Cecilie: Teo started communicating with us almost immediately after his passing. He has now directly communicated with over forty people, and as they've shared their stories, I've recorded them.

One of the most important things I've learned is that we can't heal or survive over the long run without a sense of wonder and awe.

There are plenty of teachings about how awe enriches our lives, but the simplest proof comes from Teo himself. His visitations are like tiny miracles—reminders that life is vaster than we can imagine. It's the same awe you might feel looking across the Grand Canyon or standing under a blanket of stars: a sudden, heart-bursting awareness that we're connected to something indescribably larger. Every time Teo finds a way to make contact, he gives us another dose of that wonder, fueling our spirits and guiding us to remember that we're part of something boundless and filled with mystery.

I want to share two wonderful stories of many that profoundly uplifted us when they happened because they created such a sense of awe.

Teo and his cousin were like siblings—they deeply loved each other but often irritated each other. Teo was extremely neat and precise about his clothes, while his cousin often left hers strewn about. During one of our readings, Isabella was spot-on when she said that Teo was complaining about someone staying in his room, making it messy, and drinking all the orange juice.

My first thought was: *Well, he's right about his room, where his cousin was staying, but we don't drink orange juice!* Then, I remembered that I had purchased some a few weeks earlier. An hour after this reading, Teo's cousin came home, and we asked, "Did you drink the orange juice?" She turned bright red and said, "When I came home last night, it seemed like nobody had been drinking it, so I "waterfalled" it, drinking right out of the container. And, as I was doing it, I thought Teo would be so irritated with me."

The specificity and the banality of the story made it so real—his dynamic with his cousin, the state of his room, the orange juice. It was these details that made all of us realize he was right here with us!

Another memorable session with Isabella involved a completely baffling clue: Teo showed her a Chicago Bulls trash can. We were stumped. A very opinionated sports fanatic with an astonishing depth of knowledge, we were sure it wasn't one of his teams. To be honest, I wasn't even sure what sport they played. Carolyn texted his friends about the team—no luck. I wondered if it was a metaphor or a commentary he was making. Then, exactly a week later, our friends Bob and Susie arrived from Switzerland. Susie always stayed in Teo's room and habitually brought a gift.

Sure enough, Susie reached into her backpack and pulled out a Chicago Bulls hat embroidered with Teo's name. We started screaming—so *that's* what the Bulls clue was about! We somehow had missed that they had come from Switzerland via Chicago, where they purchased the hat and had his name embroidered. Susie and Teo used to tease each other, and we realized he was telling her that the Chicago Bulls were a trash team. The Chicago Bulls were second to the bottom at the time, so he wasn't wrong. We looked at the receipt, and the purchase had been made hours before the reading.

Expanded Views of Reality

Cecilie: Sharing those stories with Teo's friends gave them the sense that he was right in the room with us.

There are many other instances in which Isabella gave us incredible insight into his state of mind. She knew from an eternal perspective how he passed, what he cared about, all these things that were quite astonishing and comforting. Time and again, her insights were backed by evidence, reinforcing for the kids that he was right there.

They also impacted us in a way I can't put into language. I honestly don't understand how other parents can go through losing a child without the sense of connectedness that we now have with our son. I don't know if I could have gotten through his transition without the reassurance that he is still with us. I have that sense because we have been through this process of rewriting our story, day by day, about being an unusual family, but an intact family, nonetheless.

Thanksgiving can be a very tough and triggering experience. But the other day, around the holiday, we were cracking each other up and reflecting on how we've always been as a family. I had this strong image that we were in a hot air balloon and wanted to take off, but these sandbags held the air balloon down. The sandbags symbolized our grief. There's a part of you that becomes accustomed to grief as an expression of love, as a way that you connect to your loved one. But then there's a part of you that asks yourself, "Can I drop the sandbag, and is that going to mean I am disconnecting from my child?"

In this vision, we conversed in the hot air balloon, and I asked Carolyn, "Can we let go of this sandbag?" Suddenly, I felt a tapping on my shoulder. It was Teo, and he was in the hot air balloon with us. He had his arms around both of us, and said, "*Let's go, you guys! This is fun*!"

It's not just a metaphor. I feel that we are moving into this place of a much more expansive lift-off after the hardest parts of this trauma, and we're not crying all day, every day. I'm thinking, *Wow! Good! Let's do this then!* Teo is multi-locating in a way none of us can understand, but it opens everything up.

Carolyn: When we share these stories, they open up our confidence to have deeper relationships where more magical things happen because we are completely unlearning and relearning our worldview. It is the most important thing we can do in the chaotic world we live in right now. We may have communication skills, but reality is much deeper than we thought. I think it will be an antidote for society, and we all need to broaden and deepen our communication to make a profound change.

Cecilie: To me, it's almost a form of child abuse not to offer this awareness to our children. During the early days after Teo's transition, Teo's friends would come over and sit outside slumped over with their masks on. I remember sharing the orange juice story in a circle with them; it greatly impacted these kids. They left the circle more buoyant. The same is true of the Chicago Bulls story. But there are so many others.

A Holistic Healing Process

Carolyn: The bottom line is that, along with Isabella's support, we're in this family business together. People may hear the word medium and not fully grasp who Isabella is and her role in helping families heal. As our healer, she is facilitating a much larger holistic healing process. We read about mediumship experiences in the media that are similar to ours. However, I believe that evidential mediums, in general, need to establish the ability and capacity to guide and heal their clients on a profoundly deep level.

We can get those direct messages from Teo and direct validations of experience. Still, Isabella is helping us expand, heal, come to terms with, interpret, and cope with one of the most impactful types of tragedies that humans end up experiencing in all these ways.

She is a holistic healer who provides clear evidence of our child's personality and how he is with us daily, gives us direct messages of healing and hope from our loved ones in Spirit, and interprets meaning. She cares deeply about us as humans and does everything she can to alleviate our suffering. I want to honor that.

So, this is my experience. Early on with Teo, I had a direct telepathic connection with our son. In one sense, it took a lot of work. In another way, it didn't. It was a very natural relationship. He's been on my mind 24/7, as children are. They're just always on your mind. You're doing this, or you're doing that, and engaging in this or that, but they're always on your mind, so that hasn't changed for me. The messages from Teo are huge and have helped me to do everything: to believe and trust. These days, he's always joking with me telepathically.

For example, earlier on, when deeply immersed in grief, I would go over his messages in my mind. I would try to work with the messages and learn from them, at one point, he said, "*Mom, nothing has ended. You've got to believe me.*" How did I know it was him I was hearing from? Partly, he spoke concisely and simply, as he always has. He wouldn't talk as much as we did, but what he did say was impactful. There is such a plaintive emotion with your child saying, "*Mom, listen to me*!"

I needed to listen to my son. I was sometimes immersed in questions like, "How could this happen? How could I have allowed this to happen?" I would be dwelling on the tragedy. I was trying to tell myself not to be ashamed. Then, Teo would cut through all that emotion and rumination and say, "*You know better than this*!"

He reminded me that I have developed capacities as a spiritual person and leader. I've dedicated myself to moving the world in a positive direction. He would say again, "*Stop. You know better than this. This is all real now. This is happening right now, right here.*" That simple phrase: "*You know better than this*!" speaks volumes. He chastised me and got my attention.

Two more examples stand out regarding how Isabella has worked with us in real-time validations. I recall one day when I'd had a rough emotional day for many reasons. I just thought, *Tomorrow's a new day! I'm going to start over tomorrow!* The next morning, Isabella texted me, saying, "Teo has a message for you. He insisted I get through to you. His message is, '*Tomorrow is a new day!*'" As I think about this support she's giving me, it's wonderful.

Teo communicates with Isabella to validate the connection, and then she texts me.

Another example happened just a week ago! I had sciatic nerve pain from a hiking injury, and she texted me asking if I was OK because Teo told her that I'd been hurt.

In addition to the stories of our conversations with Isabella that we share, their encounters with Isabella were impactful for Teo's friends. Three or four of them have had mind-blowing direct conversations with Teo through Isabella that included a lot of validations. One young man comes to mind. He had some really tough things going on in his life. Isabella texted us several times, saying that Teo was concerned and asking us to give him a message. We got the message across, and it was true and timely. Isabella has helped these now eighteen, nineteen, twenty-year-olds to understand that their friend, Teo, is with them. We have heard stories from them in which they shared many ways they have connected with Teo since he's been in Spirit. Some describe having Teo within them (living in their hearts) and guiding their lives.

Cecilie: What makes Isabella stand out among other mediums is that she can help with each person's personal pain and facilitates community building, amplifying, and expanding support for others in our circles of love beyond our circles. People need to understand this aspect of Isabella's gift as a medium. I've never read of any other medium's ability to expand their clients' depth and breadth of their lives.

I know Isabella is not coming from ego. Her strong desire is to help people. This story is just mind-boggling to me. We have a public health epidemic of loneliness, which has implications that are much broader than any of us know. Also, we have an epidemic of anxiety and depression among young people.

Isabella is an incredible example of a healer who can provide holistic therapy and a broad vision to this generation of youth and beyond who face global challenges.

Although I am open and surrounded by people, such as my mother and others who have always been open to this, I would portray myself as someone who still has a very active need for evidence. My joke has always been that I need Teo to drop a rock on my head to see and believe he's there—and he often provides the equivalent of just that. His presence has substantiated many realities for me and provided me with many material examples of impossible things.

These kids know, and subsequently, we know, in the deepest sense, that we are not alone and can ask for help. I can't tell you how transformational this has been for me. I now have what I would call a "divine faith."

I have to say repeatedly that through this experience of all the elements of working with Isabella, I have this empirical confidence that love is stronger than anything else.

My life has always been dedicated to service. This force, this field of love that Teo has, that we have for him, that he has for us, that he has for his friends, is unmistakable and is not limited by the laws of Newtonian physics. It creates these small miracles every day. Now, I understand that large miracles can happen. I work in academia, in a world that depends on language and reason and a certain kind of knowing. But the solution is not just those things. It's love. The quality of our relationships is based on a quality of love, which seems to be the field in which miracles can emerge.

Isabella guides her clients through confidence-building that doesn't manifest from Isabella's ego. This mediumistic experience with Isabella sheds light on what we're not always aware of, and she's able to validate that we all have these skills and are all communicating.

We all need someone like Isabella, who gives us the confidence to live life this other way. That is the work we need to do as humans—to survive on this planet and to be able to do it with joy. And to rediscover the multiple dimensions in which we are actually living.

Our Team

Carolyn: At the end of the day, thinking of our work with Isabella, we've been a team. We came to this relationship in the beginning when we were our most devastated, obviously desperate, and grasping for breath. There's this story about Cecilie that keeps popping into my head. As time has evolved in our communications with Teo, what he's doing, what he cares about, and mystical conversations that are more difficult to relate to in human terms are the topics.

Those have been important as well. But sometimes, he'll just shift gears. Bless Isabella. She has to keep up with Teo. One time, he shifted gears and told Cecilie to look down for the treasures. I get messages from him constantly, and when I feel despondent, he'll just say, "*Mom, look up, look up. Look at my eyes. Don't be looking around at the human world as it is. Because, to be honest, they're not going to give you any answers. Look at me. Look up."*

Cecilie: Yeah, that time he encouraged us to look down for the treasures. None of us could figure out what he was talking about, so we decided to be open to what it might mean. We thought that maybe I'd find a $100 bill or something. I forgot about it, to be honest, after that. Exactly one week later, down to the hour, I walked home from work because my bicycle had broken. It was a fifty-minute walk I'd never done before. I was just randomly zigzagging through the small Berkeley streets, most of which I had never been on before. I looked up at a new house and then looked down for a second.

There, written in the cement, on a big sidewalk, were the letters TEO, written in capital letters, exactly as he would have done. It was sort of a shock, but it was clearly the treasure he'd been discussing. That was on a Thursday. On Sunday, forty-five minutes after our usual family call ended, when I shared this story, I got a text with a photo from a friend who had been on the call. She said she was going on a walk in Oakland, and as she was sharing the "Look down for the treasure" story with her partner, they looked down, and there, carved in concrete, was Teo's name.

BECOMING A LIGHTHOUSE FOR OTHERS, A FEW STEPS BEHIND US

ISABELLA JOHNSON

Transform loss into helping others. What does that even mean? You're lost in such a tidal wave of pain that imagining a tomorrow, a week, month, or year can't even be fathomed. Here's the thing about this: grief is transient; it's never fixed. It is, at times, like a whirlpool pulling us under, and then it's a gentle lap of water rushing across our feet. It may take you under for a bit, but your head will eventually come up again. That is a promise.

Some people are very proactive in those moments. They don't want their experience to be wasted, whether it's to share their loved ones with others or simply make a change in the world in some way to honor their experience. We can do great things in this space. We can become a lighthouse for others a few steps behind us, just as this family did, even in the midst of unimaginable loss.

CHRIS RYAN AND CYN COLIP

"Our son is working to keep the healing process going."

Chris and Cyn: We have a son in Spirit, Sean Gabriel Ryan. Our only son, Sean, transitioned on September 7, 2021, at the age of twenty-three from Fentanyl poisoning. He was just two weeks shy of his twenty-forth birthday.

As we navigated our way through this intense emotional crisis, we began doing research into the afterlife. "Where *is* Sean?"

Sean Gabriel Ryan

We attended a Helping Parents Heal conference in Phoenix in August 2022. At one of the conference's many medium gallery readings, Sean "connected." It was our first time feeling his presence (and humor).

Chris: Working with insightful evidential mediums has been very helpful in our healing process. Several readings from various sources have connected with our son in Spirit, with varying levels of success. I can't say that we have a definitive, singular experience of what changed in us after the reading with Isabella. There's an accumulation of connections with our son that is very validating and comforting for us. Isabella was really, really accurate, and my reading with her was an excellent experience. But it wasn't necessarily my first reading with Isabella that changed or shifted something for me.

Cyn: Isabella's reading was one of the first I'd had after Sean's transition. So, for me, it really did make a difference. I was open to her. I want to pinpoint how and why I sought out Isabella in particular. She was interviewed as part of a Helping Parents Heal podcast. I was impressed by who she was and how she did her practice. I immediately resonated with her—the humor, the warmth, but more specifically, because she had gone through the same experience of losing a child. So, I felt this was someone who knew intimately what it felt like, which proved to be true.

What was so helpful on her podcast was that she spoke about the fact that she had no longer wanted to be here after her daughter passed. Since she had shared those feelings during the podcast, I could share my similar feelings more easily when speaking to her one-on-one.

It wasn't just the reading; it was also me telling her how much I honored her for being so honest because I was in the throes of that when I talked to her. I had never expected to experience such overwhelming and excruciating pain. I didn't want to be here anymore. I felt, "I want out. I just want out of this." So, for her to shift the reading into having a one-on-one conversation with me and somewhat normalizing those feelings was huge. It was *huge*. It gave me an open space to share and know that it was a safe place. Truly, she got it. *She got it.*

Chris: I can build on that. Isabella's been one of the most empathetic and sensitive mediums we've known. She understands those emotions of not wanting to be here. When she connects with our son, she gets emotional, which overwhelms her. I feel like Sean's with us at that moment. A flood of emotion comes through her from the other side that I can see and hear, making it very powerful for us. She has a very tender heart, which comes through in her empathy. It's a real connection, an emotional connection.

Cyn: It was a very different kind of feeling with Isabella. In the past, with other medium readings, our takeaway was more like, "Oh, I can believe this. It's a curiosity and kind of fun. Let's see what happens." In contrast, my reading with Isabella came from desperation. I had such a different mindset when getting the reading.

There's a need there: "Where's my kid? Where's my kid?" So, for her to offer up a pathway was instrumental. It didn't take the grief away but gave me a moment to breathe. I could breathe again. And it lasts a little while. It's not like when the reading is over, and you instantly return to the heaviness. It lightens a load of grief for a while.

Chris: It's worth saying that Cyn had the first reading with Isabella, and I wasn't there, so it wasn't a couples reading. This was in the summer of 2022. Our son had only been in Spirit for nine months, and we were early in the process. My first reading with Isabella was in December 2023, so there had been over a year between the two readings.

Chris: Since my first reading was after Cyn's, one thing that stuck out was that she felt that our son, Sean, had more to tell us. Isabella offered Cyn a complimentary session—not necessarily as a reading, but to delve deeper into the work needed. She offered to do a Soul Reading with Cyn, but it turned into something different, and I'll let her explain that.

Even after the time gap between our two readings, some words or a specific phrase came through from Sean in both of our readings, which made me think that not only did she lock-in, but it provided proof beyond reproach. Some of the phrasing and personality around the purpose of his being in our lives were spot-on between our separate readings. You just wouldn't connect the dots that way unless you were truly connecting with Sean's spirit.

Chris: She spoke about the purpose of his being in our lives. Sean was twenty-three when he passed. He had struggled with drug use and some alcohol through his teenage years. Through speaking with Isabella, it became clear to both of us that he had accomplished his mission and had come here and done what he needed to do. His mission was to express and share unconditional love, which includes service to others and to teach us. Cyn always said, "He's my best teacher."

Part of what alarmed us while he was here on earth and caused us to ask was, "Why is he going under bridges and hanging out with homeless people?" All we saw was that he was hanging out with the wrong crowd, but what came through with Isabella was his being of service and learning compassion and expressing acceptance with these people, people who were looking at him and saying, "Why are you here? You go home to a family. You have a roof over your head. Why are you hanging out with us?"

He was relating to people who seemed to be outsiders or indigent. Isabella used the quote from the Bible to help describe Sean's motivation: "Even to the least of these…" in both of our readings. This is a quote from Jesus about serving people experiencing poverty. The fact that Sean was ministering to people and willing to be generous "even to the least of these" is part of what he was here to do. This was very powerful for Isabella when she heard this and powerful for us, as well.

And, again, that quote came through for both of us, with a significant length of time between each of us having a personal reading with Isabella.

It gave us a lot of comfort knowing that Sean was special in that way, that he had come here, that he had had a profound love for us—which was kind of a remarkable thing for us—not that

Cyn Colip and Chris Ryan

kids don't have a love for their parents. Still, there was something unique about the depth of his connection to us on a soul level.

His unusual example gave a good sense of Sean's mission here and helped us better understand why he was ready to leave early.

Cyn: The whole idea of his choosing us and that we benefit in terms of his being of service to others and allowing others to be of service to him is a lesson for us that we carry forward, not being judgmental and having compassion. I always said he was my greatest teacher, and he continues to be.

So, little glimpses like that keep him so present in our lives, and "Yep, there are more lessons to learn." He just went ahead first. He went home first. We'll keep learning our lessons. We're staying awake and keep learning.

I see Isabella as a conduit for us to keep learning our lessons.

Another aspect of this process with Isabella is that she empowers her clients to use their conversations with her as a springboard and encourages us to do our own investigating rather than creating a dynamic in which we're depending on her.

That was part of my question for her: *How can I continue this?* And she was very generous, suggesting, "Here, try this, try that," to develop your connection.

I appreciate that she was generous with her information about mediumship. She said, "Be your own medium. You can do this!"

One of the methods that she shared with me, which she has found helpful, is creating a completely dark and quiet space. She had done this while participating in a research project in which she scored in the top 97% of mediums in accuracy. It was something that fast-tracked her to quiet her mind and connect. She mentioned other helpful strategies, including writing, which I've also found to be very helpful.

I just appreciate somebody in her position encouraging me, saying, "You can do this too. You don't need me!"

Chris: There are many good mediums who are focused on the details of the evidence that they can provide. Isabella can provide detailed evidence, but she also taps into our son's emotional feelings. We had a real sense of Sean's personality and love when engaged in sessions with Isabella. How she could play around with his spirit and communicate his personality was truly helpful. Through this process, she explored areas of discussion that she thought might be helpful, while he was often insistent on focusing on the areas that he was interested in. She was quite willing to be flexible with him in this way. We really got a more genuine sense that we were all together, right here with us, as opposed to someone just ticking off a list of evidence.

Cyn: Part of that was not only the deep emotion of sadness but also the humor Sean brought through, which would have been our kid! He was joking around and laughing during this intense time. That's huge in terms of lightening the load of grief, being able to tap into that lightness, and having moments of joy within the reading.

Chris: One of the things that came straight out of his mouth, or spirit, was that we struggled with his addiction. We had him in the house. We had him in rehab. We had him in sober living. We had him back in the house. He went back and forth. One of the things he said through Isabella was, "I would have kicked me out, too."

That was good to hear because it let us off the hook a little bit. It gave us hope as a parent. You want to know, as a parent, "Did we do the right thing? Did we make his death more imminent by forcing him out from under our protection and care?" A lot of parents do that. They keep their kids protected in this little cocoon and keep them sick all their lives. We couldn't handle it.

We had decided it was too crazy for us and asked him to leave. He did. He agreed. And we were very proud of him to have the strength to do that and not hold it over us and be guilting us. It was the beginning of a healing period, actually, when he did leave, it began a path for us to heal our relationship.

He is guiding us to this day. Before his passing, we both had a belief system that there's more to our lives than this earthly existence. We knew there was some sort of an afterlife. Certainly, Sean's passing catapulted us into not just believing, but to knowing.

Chris: Initially, after the death of a child, you are consumed with a sense of fear: "Where is my kid?" "What did I do?" "Did I screw up?" This is a crisis of grief as a parent. However, over time, with the help of Spirit, you feel comforted; you know that you haven't said goodbye, and don't have to say goodbye.

Cyn: Self-blame doesn't help anybody.

Chris: One of the things that Sean shared with Isabella and that she brought forward was that he was so proud of me. Sean relayed that there were other kids and other children with him in Spirit and that they were excited about helping them tell their stories. We can do that through the Helping Fathers Heal group, an affiliate group to Helping Parents Heal.

Isabella would never have known this, but I was writing a book; a collection of stories from twenty-five of the fathers in our Helping Fathers Heal group who are all talking about their grief and their personal healing experiences.

Isabella relayed that Sean told her it was a group of about twenty-five. He said, "It's mostly about boys. There are only seven girls." I went back and counted the chapters. There are seven female and eighteen male children.

The fact that Sean is so proud and the kids are excited to share their stories made me feel connected. And again, that's such a big part of our healing, not only connecting with our son but connecting with other people who we can help; people who get it and understand what we're going through.

There's just a lot more magic in our lives now than before.

My book, *Helping Fathers Heal: Grief, Hope and Our Search for Connection*, was released just prior to the Helping Parents Heal convention in August 2024. Maintaining the father's voice was important to us as we worked on this project.

Cyn: That's something that Isabella picked up on, something you repeatedly told me. "I feel like the kids are with me. When I'm helping Chris proof this book, I feel like they're all gathering around me and helping me."

Chris: Other mediums have also mentioned that the children are gathered around me, helping me with this project.

Cyn: The kids are excited!

Chris: Isabella has brought us peace, healing, and connection. It's more than just a parlor trick; being in a gallery reading and having a few nuggets thrown your way is lovely. But there's a difference when you feel immersed in the same Spirit, your child, who is with you right there.

Cyn: I recently reviewed the two readings that I had with Isabella. I was reminded that she had offered to return and do a Soul Plan reading about a month after my first reading.

It just so happened that the day we had arranged to do this had been a tough morning for me, as I'd had to say goodbye to one of my dearest friends, who was dying of cancer. She was no longer conscious. She was in the Midwest, in Ohio, and her husband held the phone to her ear. A few hours later, I'm just wracked with emotion. It was nine months after Sean had passed, and I was saying goodbye to one of my closest friends.

The timeliness of having that meeting set up with Isabella was so crucial. On her side, the plan was to do a soul-planning reading for me, as I mentioned. When we started our meeting, she said she'd been up since 6:00 a.m. and my son was coming through. That's not what she was expecting. That's not what it was supposed to look like, but he insisted that she had to get something through to me.

She said he was immovable. During her readings, Isabella sometimes tries to clear the way of those trying to get her attention so that she can connect with guides. On this particular morning, she'd tried maneuvering Sean out of the way, but he was insistent. "Nope! This has to happen today!" It was so poignant that I got his message that morning. It was clear to me that something else was at play.

So, she read what he had dictated to her. It was a love letter to Mom. It was huge; it was what I needed to hear after going through this again, another massive loss in my life. My friend passed away the next day.

To this day, this letter continues to provide me with healing. It is something that I will treasure forever. It is such a tangible piece of healing.

Reviewing my reading with Isabella reaffirms that my son is still here and working on my behalf to keep the healing process going. I am eternally grateful for that piece of evidence.

Chris: We didn't spend a lot of time on proof during our discussion today, and there are more examples we could have offered; however, the message of Sean's dedication to service and the empathy that Isabella brought through helped us better understand his mission in life and why he was able to leave when he did. It was very healing.

Cyn: The experience with Isabella allows us to keep putting one foot in front of the other and moving forward. It gives us the space to breathe and supports us as we continue on our healing path.

SOMETIMES YOU'RE LUCKY TO FIND YOUR PERSON EARLY

ISABELLA JOHNSON

Partnerships are tricky; we evolve and grow, and rarely does that occur at the same pace as the person we are with. As the years turn into decades and we've built a home and family life with our partner, our differences become less pronounced and obvious. Annoyances may remain, but we have begun to see ourselves as one unit.

Then the unimaginable happens: your partner goes home to Spirit, leaving you with an incredible emptiness that morphs into a chasm. What I find most comforting is that although we experience a physical separation, our loved ones are closer than a breath away, and as you'll read below, they are still very intertwined with events in our lives. There is no true separation beyond what our eyes can perceive.

LESLIE ZUCZEK

"My sessions evolved into a deeper interaction with André, more about what he was doing, his spiritual growth, and his beliefs."

Our son, André, was 15 years old when he decided to experiment with LSD with a couple of his friends on March 18, 2017. He had little understanding of what he was taking; unfortunately, things went terribly wrong. He ended up on the balcony, and as the police were arriving, they witnessed him fall three stories. He was immediately taken to the hospital, had surgery, and remained in a coma until he was pronounced dead on March 20, 2017.

Three generations gather from left to right: Jean-Marc Zuczek, Leslie Zuczek, André Zuczek, Fay Janzen, Ziggy Lowell Janzen (Leslie's parents).

Our foundation collapsed beneath us, and my husband, Jean-Marc, and I joined a club no parent wanted to join. We both had a solid spiritual background and understood this was a soul contract and his time.

We subsequently had several experiences after his transition where André told us he was still with us. He tapped into anyone here who was open to hearing him. André wanted us to know how sorry he was and that his passing was unintentional. He has continued to let us know how much he loves us.

While we had a good understanding of the afterlife, we had never really explored much regarding it. Before André died, I was a hospice social worker and a bereavement counselor. It seems that line of work helped prepare me for this significant loss and gave me a lot of support, as many of my friends are in the hospice business. Who better to have support from than friends who are in the hospice business?

I already had a belief system, but I wasn't that interested in what happens to you after transitioning because I didn't have a significant loss until that point. However, when our son transitioned, we became consumed with learning more. We read or listened to Michael Newton's *Journey of Souls* and other books that helped us refine and deepen our understanding.

About five months after André transitioned, our friend bought us tickets to a gallery reading, and, unsurprisingly, our son came in first. This was our very first experience communicating through a medium. André was quite determined and ignored the medium's process of spirits waiting in line, which the medium acknowledged while, at the same time, laughing at his rebelliousness. His personality shone through! After that, Jean-Marc and I joined a spirit circle and continued communicating with André through mediums. Several mediums helped me get through the worst part of my grief.

Jean-Marc and I also belong to Helping Parents Heal (HPH). In 2018, I asked Mark Ireland, the cofounder of HPH, who certifies mediums, for a recommendation. He highly recommended Isabella Johnson. I wanted someone who could connect with my son in Spirit to help my parents, Fay and Lowell Janzen, who were having difficulties dealing with his death.

I arranged for my parents to have a reading from Isabella. I sat in on the session as my parents were new to this. My dad is very conservative and somewhat skeptical, but my mom was more open to it as I had shared many of our experiences with her.

I wanted to assist them in understanding that the communication I was currently having with my son, André, was real and valid to experience being with my son in Spirit and to know that my son, while not in the physical, was very much present in our lives.

During the session, Isabella immediately picked up on how André had passed. She knew that it was an unexpected death. She mentioned how he had no experience with this drug and was with friends who also took LSD. She said that it was a bad trip and specified that the drugs didn't take his life, but the fall did. Isabella also mentioned that my parents were concerned that the accident was on purpose. They admitted to thinking about that yet had never mentioned it to each other.

Isabella relayed to us, from André's perspective, that he had fallen and hit his head and that it took his breath away. At first, he didn't know if it was real or if he was tripping. He experienced no suffering or lingering during this time. He wanted to let us know he experienced no pain. Even though he was pronounced dead a few days later, he led Isabella to the location of the fall. That was where he had left his body and transitioned to the other side. This confirmed what I had believed; that he was already out of his body then.

Isabella relayed our son's personality with his great sense of humor and spoke about his compassion. She relayed his visits with Grandma and Grandpa, how they spoiled him, and how much he appreciated all they did for him. He even ratted out my mom, letting us know how she let him drive and blast his rap music in her sporty convertible. He wanted to thank her for how much he enjoyed his time with them.

There were so many accurate details that my dad couldn't dispute the information that André was communicating to us. André wanted Isabella to emphasize that it was an accident, a flawed experiment that went very wrong.

During this reading, André also brought up that he had signed a contract with the Dare program at his school. During that time, he had worn a t-shirt that included warnings not to do drugs. André said that in ninth grade, he didn't feel like he fit in. Overall, Isabella picked up that he was a regular teen going through teen angst and that he thought that his taking LSD was a horrible mistake.

This session was so full of evidence that Isabella couldn't possibly have made up. The session was extremely helpful and brought comfort to my parents and me. For me, confirming that he left his body when he fell and didn't experience pain was comforting. For my parents, so many memories were established, and conversing with him comforted them.

Father Shares Poignant Moments

My husband, Jean-Marc, and I have been through this journey together, sharing many poignant moments. He reminded me recently of one of the most meaningful, which I want to share, in his words. Here is his account:

> On the sunny afternoon of Christmas Eve, 2018, my wife and I decided to visit and enjoy the very special energy of our local Bell Rock in Sedona and took an impromptu selfie with the Bell Rock in the background. We posted it on Facebook with our Christmas wishes and headed home shortly afterward.
>
> Later that same day, one of our Facebook friends, who's a photographer, reached out to my wife, Leslie, with a private text containing a black-and-white version of that very same picture, but with the luminosity levels adjusted just to reveal the shocking presence of a clear head, face and shoulder outline in the upper right corner of the image where the sun was peeking in the frame!
>
> We hadn't noticed any of this in our original picture and were amazed at this outcome! While this outline didn't specifically look like André, we were quite certain that it was André's way of wanting to be included in our "Christmas Best Wishes" picture for all our Facebook friends and family. We were, once again,

The Zuczek's visit to Bell Rock in Sedona, Arizona, on Christmas eve, 2018. André later confirmed, during a gallery reading in 2019, that his image appeared in the photo.

both quite moved, amazed, and grateful at his continued efforts to remind us of his continued non-physical presence in our lives. Still, we decided to keep this extraordinary experience strictly to ourselves and mentioned it to no one for the time being.

About two months later, in February 2019, we heard Isabella was about to do an in-person gallery reading at the monthly Helping Parents Heal meeting in Phoenix. We at once decided to attend, and soon after we were driving down from Sedona to Phoenix to that end. During the drive, my wife jokingly said to me that because André had already popped up so many times before in prior private and public medium readings, including Isabella's, she didn't want to deprive other parents of Isabella's limited time, and didn't expect a full visit from André on this occasion. Specifically addressing herself to both André and me out loud with a knowing smile, she said a simple "Hi, Mom!" would be enough.

An hour later or so, we were sitting in the fully packed room with many other parents. Isabella was walking around the room, delivering messages with her usual loving, compassionate touch, and remarkable accuracy. As the session was getting close to ending, and Leslie and I had likely surrendered the hope to hear from André, Isabella suddenly looked directly at us from across the room and, without any introduction, said out loud: "*Hi, Mom! Hi Mom! Hi Mom!*" three times in a row!

My wife and I looked at each other in delight and immediately laughed out loud at André's wonderful sense of humor in fulfilling his mom's tiny wish uttered just an hour or so ago in the car! But then Isabella returned to the stage, kept talking about André for a bit, and asked: "Did something happen recently about a picture or something … in the Red Rocks?" We immediately shared the whole picture "appearance" with her, to which she replied: "He keeps saying "*I DID THAT! I DID THAT*!" Needless to say, we and everyone else in the room were quite stunned and amazed at this sharing, which was just one more remarkable demonstration of Isabella's wonderful gift and abilities. This will forever remain one of our all-time favorite interactions with André through Isabella! Forever grateful.

—Jean-Marc Zuczek

Supporting My Mother's Journey

Later, I attended one of the Helping Parents Heal Zoom meetings. Isabella first brought up André and then tuned in to my mom, who was in the hospital then. André was sitting next to my mom, watching out for her. This gave me great relief since we had not been able to visit my mom while she was in the hospital for three weeks because of all the COVID restrictions. Isabella was so sensitive to the situation that she told me to call her after the group meeting so she could talk more privately. She does that for others, too. Isabella is so amazing! She is so loving and compassionate.

During the private conversation, I told her I was planning on placing my mom in hospice and having her come home. Isabella encouraged me to bring her home sooner rather than later because she wasn't sure how long my mom would be able to hang on. So, I initiated the process earlier than I had planned. I was so grateful for Isabella's advice. I believe if she had to stay in the hospital any longer than she did, she probably would have transitioned there.

The doctor had kept encouraging us to do curative care even though she was dying. I chose instead to make arrangements for her to have hospice care at home. I decided to act quickly because Isabella encouraged me to do it right away. When she came home from the hospital, before she got in the door, my mom told me she didn't want any treatment that would keep her here longer. She was ready and looking forward to being with André. She had been in the hospital for three weeks, and I felt that our doctor was not comfortable with the dying process.

My mom transitioned in May 2020, about a week after coming home. My mom might not have held on had we waited any longer. It was a tremendous gift that she had given me because we had that time together. I feel that the session with Isabella helped her to let go.

A few months after my mom passed, I had another session with Isabella. The session was focused on my mom. It was so amazing and went so beyond evidential. It was an intimate conversation with my mom, who expressed her regrets about our relationship. It was so deep that Isabella and I were both crying! It was a conversation my mom and I could not have while she was in the physical. I was so grateful for this session. It gave me so much closure and was very healing.

Isabella is a compassionate person who is far above any other medium. I've had incredible experiences during my many sessions with her. Although we no longer needed Isabella to provide evidential information, my sessions evolved into a deeper interaction with André, more about what he was doing, his spiritual growth, and his beliefs.

I also learned about grief from Isabella, hearing about her own experiences. She gave me hope as I was struggling. She has shared different stories about her own life and her vast expertise with families who were grieving about those family members who have transitioned to the other side.

For instance, in the fourth year following a transition, Isabella often sees people shifting gears, able to move on from their grief. Before that, grief tended to be all-consuming.

Then, as time passed, she shared this meaningful story about her mother. When Isabella was particularly grieving, her mom tried to console her by sharing that when a china plate gets broken in Japan, they take it and get it mended with gold. Then, it becomes more valuable and more beautiful than it ever was. Isabella shared that she eventually understood what her mom was trying to convey.

Isabella said: "I look at the tapestry of my life and am just grateful. I wouldn't have this compassion towards other parents if I didn't have the experience of losing my daughter. I wouldn't understand what widows feel if I didn't have this experience. It's made me a better person and a better medium. I'm just so grateful."

There are just little gems I continually learn from her, which have been so helpful in my process, aside from the readings.

Now, when working in person with Isabella, I have these deep conversations with my son. It helps me have that connection and grow. I now have no interest in seeing any other mediums than her.

These days, I can see André. Even though I can communicate with him myself, I enjoy talking to him with Isabella acting as a conduit, because it's more evident when she speaks on his behalf during our sessions.

I'll see an image of André or feel him within me when I'm doing yoga. I have a lot of experiences on my own, but with Isabella, it's just confirming, and I'm having a two-way conversation. Isabella has encouraged me to have confidence in being able to hear him, and I am forever grateful for her ongoing support.

ALWAYS BE LISTENING

ISABELLA JOHNSON

Everyone has intuition. *Everyone.* Sometimes we listen, and sometimes we do not. When we are broken open by grief, our minds desperately search out clues to make "it" make sense. Intuition kicks into overdrive. We put away things that no longer serve us, a new paradigm opens, and we step across that threshold, never to return. Our life transforms.

You will find talents previously untapped, and you'll find courage previously unimagined, and slowly, life will evolve into something beyond our wildest dreams. Our loved ones in Spirit guide us to these things, sometimes very loudly; other times, it's nothing more than a thought or dream we can't push away.

Life can become bigger than we ever imagined, and it will be if we trust the process.

MICHELLE CRAWFORD-GONZALES

"I didn't know before Eric's passing that we are all born with gifts. Once he said, "Mom, you're so gifted!" And I said, "No, you're gifted!" He said, "No, you're gifted!"

My son, Eric, passed away about eight years ago. His journey to the other side was entirely unexpected. My daughter, Cassie, hadn't heard from her brother, so she called me and contacted the police, who found his body in an apartment complex. Later, I identified his body.

I was in so much pain. I hid for a year. The second year, I was so numb and didn't want to be around anybody. I felt no joy, and my daughter was worried about me. She brought my granddaughter to me and she snapped me out of it.

Eric and Michelle Gonzales

After that, I started seeing and feeling again. I started listening to quantum physicists' lectures about consciousnesses and realized I was a sensitive empath. I watched and read everything I could about the subject and learned that Earth is a school and we are here to expand ourselves.

Isabella and I first connected in 2020. I saw her during a Helping Parents Heal Zoom meeting, which I'd learned about after exploring the documentary series *Life to Afterlife: Mom Can You Hear Me?* I had invited my daughter, Cassie, to join me, and after hearing Isabella Johnson speak, my daughter texted me: *Mom, I have to have a reading with her!*

Cassie set up the meeting for herself and Isabella. As the meeting started, Isabella asked, "Wait a minute, does your mother write books?" She said, "Yes," and Isabella asked if she had a brother who had passed. My daughter said, "Yes," and Isabella said, "Your mother needs to be present." So, she rescheduled for a few days later, and my daughter and I had the reading with Isabella.

Isabella knew everything that was going on. No one could have known the things she revealed in the session. During this first meeting, I learned Isabella had four sons and a daughter. I had four daughters and a son. We both have had a child that has transitioned to the other side.

Several people gathered at my sister's house during a second reading. Isabella said, "Your son is out on the balcony, and now he has his hands on the window." Soon after the meeting ended, we went to check, and sure enough, there were fresh fingerprints on the window.

As time has passed, I've thrown myself into the spiritual realm. I've talked to Eric on the other side through Isabella. I didn't know before Eric's passing that we are all born with gifts. Once he said, *"Mom, you're so gifted!"* And I said, "No, you're gifted!" He said, *"No, you're gifted!"* Eric encouraged me to write. I decided to go ahead and write a book, even though I had never even taken a creative writing class or listened to friends and acquaintances who had encouraged me to write before this time.

I've now written books, using the pen name, M. L. Blackburn, about our connection to heaven and how angels work to save the world.

After I met Isabella, she was so generous with her time, would give me pep talks, and raise my spirits. She is so connected. Her gift is beyond imagination. Isabella has taught me so much. Knowing her has been a beautiful experience. Without her, I wouldn't be on the path I'm on. She is one of the most gifted women I know in mediumship.

As we grow up, we tend to believe what our parents have raised us to believe. As we mature, we will likely develop our own spiritual lens. I also believe a soul connection exists between us and our children. Eric has helped me develop my spiritual lens from the other side. If he hadn't passed, I would probably be living with my blinders on. But now, I see things as they are and accept and believe in what I see spiritually.

I always tell my girls, "We're a spiritual being having a physical experience."

There are so many things on earth that are not just physical. For example, I've seen birds disappear and reappear, letting me know we're not just physical beings. I've grown to accept what I perceive instead of pushing it aside. Some say, "The eyes are the windows to the soul." I think that the soul has windows that we don't understand.

Gonzales family siblings

There have been times since my son transitioned to the other side that he has imprinted. Once, I saw him as I walked through the bedroom into the kitchen, and it suddenly dawned on me that I had seen my son. I walked back around and smiled. Then he dissipated, like steam. Another time, when I was at a stoplight, I glanced back and saw him skateboarding, which he used to do before he died.

I also feel that we're often not equipped to handle the tragedies in our lives. This can be seen when we instinctively call to God for help at these times. As we tune in to our souls following these events, we understand more.

I'm not a religious person, and I'm not a part of any group or church. The three things that I believe in are: each person provides a structure for one's faith; our belief system is, in fact, our faith; and we are all connected to the heavenly Father. Prayer is powerful. I call God the heavenly father, creator of all things. He is the Father in heaven.

I know my son is OK now. Everything is good now.

CONNECTIONS BIGGER THAN TIME

ISABELLA JOHNSON

The word soulmate is overused. We tend to romanticize them and imagine the ease that will come in every aspect of life with that individual. That is rarely an accurate description of a soulmate.

A soulmate can be a partner, a child, or a parent. It's a connection that feels differently than others; there is a depth and an innate knowing that, for whatever reason, we are committed to experiencing events in life together. We simply know that on a cellular level, we have lost ourselves.

No bonds are ever truly broken, but when our "person" transitions, the loss may feel like we've lost ourselves. These particular people seem to be extra diligent in reminding us of these facts.

The emptiness of their presence can be transcended into a deep, abiding connection.

LINDA

"People! Let me tell you something. I'm not lost! You didn't lose me! I'm right here. Stop saying I'm lost. I'm not. Think about life now and how it will be in a few months."

Throughout my ten-year journey since my son in Spirit, SP, transitioned to the other side, I have met with ten or eleven different mediums, including Isabella. My readings with Isabella never cease to amaze me.

I was beyond devastated after the transition of my son. He worked for the government, and I was told by the authorities investigating his death that he had taken his own life. I am intuitive, and I knew that there was something suspicious about the information they quickly gave me. A self-inflicted death is still considered questionable until all the evidence is collected. This did not happen. His was an open-and-shut case with no formal inquiries.

I needed to start my own investigation because every time I asked questions, I was met with the same narrative, and the phone conversations ended with more confusion than answers.

Immediately after my son transitioned, I spoke with two other excellent mediums, but they only relayed that SP kept repeating, "*I didn't do it, Mom.*" However, they were unable to give me details of his death.

Fortunately, less than a year later, I was invited to participate in a documentary with Isabella Johnson. When I met her, she looked away from me and said, "Oh, your son's here." She described his physical appearance to a tee and laughed at his dry sense of humor.

How was it possible that she was so incredibly accurate about not only his physical appearance but his personality as well? I inquired about getting a reading with her, and she was kind enough to schedule one within a few weeks.

As she contacted SP, Isabella took notes on a yellow pad, and right in the middle she had written: "Coverup." That gave me chills, which is my sign of validation. Isabella immediately began explaining the details of his passing and why. There were a myriad of emotions running through my body at the same time. I was stunned by her accuracy regarding SP—his personality, and the personal conversations he and I had before his transition. I was furious that the authorities were lying to me, and, at the same time, I was relieved that he was thriving on the other side. He assured me he would always be with our family.

The most significant moment of my first reading with Isabella was the yellow pad with the word "Coverup" circled repeatedly. As she continued with our reading, the details began to unravel, and the puzzle pieces began to fit together perfectly.

SP and I had a personal conversation about trivets the day before he died. We were both laughing at the word, and he sent me a picture of a wall of trivets on his phone as a joke. Isabella picked up on that. He was also a big guy, and we had joked about him wanting a beach bike with a basket and a bell. She also brought that up. Through my tears, I had a smile on my face because I knew beyond a shadow of a doubt that this was my amazing son.

She also went on to relay many details about my (now-ex) husband, who, unfortunately, remained skeptical about the reason for SP's death. He thought that my insistence of a cover-up was my way of coping with SP's death. My daughter was also suspicious about her brother's passing being self-inflicted, despite evidence to the contrary. I believe it was easier for my son's dad to accept that narrative and move on because he had worked for the same organization years earlier. Even after a reading with Isabella with validations that shocked him, he still clung tightly to his narrative about SP's death. We will all meet again after our passing, and wounds from this lifetime will be healed.

My experiences with Isabella have validated what I have known all along. After death, we change frequencies and communicate differently. I've studied quantum physics and have an understanding from an intellectual perspective. However, my perspective changed from believing to knowing without a shadow of a doubt, through communicating with those on the other side, including my late father.

I have been so fortunate to be able to communicate with SP through dream visitations and signs, as well as the time he gave me a hug. I could feel his arms wrapped around me, and I could even kiss his arm before he disappeared.

This is not to say I don't miss his physical presence. I absolutely do, every day. I remember waking up that first couple of months and saying, "Oh my God, I'm not gonna do anything (to harm myself), but how can I go through another day without him here?" It seemed to be an insurmountable task that I wasn't sure I could endure.

At one point, SP asked me to stop saying I "lost" him. He said in an almost demanding voice: "*People! Let me tell you something. I'm not lost! You didn't lose me! I'm right here. Stop saying I'm lost. I'm not. Think about life now and how it will be in a few months.*"

Isabella has validated that our souls are intertwined. SP helped me move beyond my feelings of depression after his passing. He changed my mindset from "It's another day without him," to "I'm one day closer to being reunited with my son." I wake up with a positive outlook because I know we don't die, and I still have work to do before I cross over.

Not long ago, I had a list of all the things I wanted to discuss with Isabella during my reading, and she methodically went down the list without me even saying a word. I still make a list, mostly so I will remember what I want to discuss, not because she won't answer every question before I even ask.

I was part of Helping Parents Heal's 'Caring Listener' program, which is available 24 hours a day. I've been able to discuss my journey and hopefully hold the hands of parents whose children have moved to the other side as they explore their journey, just as mine was held in the beginning.

Isabella volunteers her time to this organization, as well. She strives to provide as many validations as she can for the parents. I think she's incredibly generous, which speaks volumes about her soul's mission while she is here in the physical realm.

I've dealt a lot with parents for obvious reasons in the ten years since my son transitioned. The most challenging question is how to find words to define our situation.

When a spouse passes, you become a widow or widower. Parents transition, and the description of orphans comes to mind. However, there are no words for a parent who has lost a child. The pain is so intense that any terminology would not do it justice.

It helped me tremendously to write a book about the loss of my son. I've included a chapter in which I offered the readers as many resources as possible. Ironically, as my editor reviewed my book, she asked me about Chapter 13 since we had not discussed it beforehand. I called her immediately and told her I did not recall writing Chapter 13, yet there it was! Obviously, Spirit had more to say.

Isabella has helped me tremendously in many ways, even encouraging me as I decided if I should publish my work. When parents ask me how to connect with their children, I suggest not to try so hard. I just ask that they be ready to receive because each child will communicate differently as they know their child best.

SP and I love Isabella; she has brought us closer than ever. My perspective of death has radically changed, and my mission is to show others that the continuation of life is not only possible, it is *real*.

LIFE'S SYNCHRONICITIES

ISABELLA JOHNSON

The people we didn't know we needed in life show up when they should; the problem is that they never seem to stay long enough. When we lose someone, we also lose hope for a moment. We feel they've traveled to a location impossible to find and wonder if we will see them again. Do they know that we love them, that we are struggling with their absence? Will we ever be okay again? Let me assure you: once in Spirit, we are closer than you can imagine. We know every thought and emotion of those still here in the physical experience, and we want nothing more than to let you know one thing. You are *never* alone.

JOANN REDA

"This experience has completely changed my life, and I am now at peace."

At the time of my husband Andrew's passing, we were living in Baltimore, Maryland, where I had been running a daycare for twenty-seven years. Before we were married, we were not necessarily close friends. At that time, I already had four children. After we married, he took those four children in and raised them as his own.

Then, about five years ago, he was diagnosed with Chronic Lymphocytic Leukemia (CLL). His doctor told him not to worry about it, that most people die *with* it, not *because* of it. He just had to have his blood checked every few months. He was fine. Then, in the spring of 2019, his leg started hurting badly. They said he had Richter's Transformation (RS), which is defined as the transformation of chronic lymphocytic leukemia (CLL)

Joann and Andrew Reda

into an aggressive lymphoma, most commonly Diffuse large B-cell lymphoma (DLBCL).

The doctor said that he could get a stem cell transplant and everything would be fine, but the nurses at the hospital told us that he would only live for two months. That's what happened. He died within two months.

When Andrew passed away, I was already retired and receiving Social Security benefits, but not the total amount. I couldn't afford to stay in Baltimore. We had planned to retire and move to Hampstead, North Carolina in December, and he passed away in July. My son George was a Marine stationed there, and we vacationed there every year. We loved it there, so I decided to move and follow our plan. Two of my kids moved there with me after selling my house in Baltimore and buying one in Hampstead. I had gone to hospice grief counseling, and it hadn't helped me at all. They did nothing for me. Then, I saw information about Isabella on Facebook. I read up on her, watched some videos, and decided to talk to this lady. I had a really strong feeling about her, that she was the real deal. So, I had a meeting with her, and the minute I got on the Zoom call with her, I felt completely at ease. She understood everything. She was caring and compassionate. I got an instant good vibe from her.

"Look for Flowers."

I only had a couple of questions, which I asked, and she answered. I wanted to know if Andrew was OK and if he was afraid. She put me at ease about that. She answered everything. Isabella told me many things that no one else would have known. She even quoted him. One thing she told me was that he was sending signs. He said, "*Look for flowers.*" It was January! It's cold in January, even here!

After I got off the phone with her, I went out to the porch, where there was a bush with one flower. Now, every January, there's another flower. This year, there are four flowers on this one bush. There aren't any other flowers around. It's January! It will be four years since Andrew transitioned in July.

I've talked with Isabella twice. After talking with her, I'm at peace, knowing that he is OK and watching over us. I learned that his mother, who has also transitioned, swooped him up when he passed. She said my father, who has also transitioned, was saluting a young man during the reading. I think he was saluting my son George, the Marine. I was torn about moving, and Andrew told me I did the right thing. This gave me confidence.

Family Members Receive Surprising Information

My grandson also talked to her, and my sister just spoke to Isabella. My sister had been very skeptical before talking to Isabella. She made it very clear: "I won't tell her anything unless she tells me something first!" After her reading with Isabella, my sister said, "Isabella is fantastic and shared many details she couldn't have possibly known about."

My grandson and his wife had miscarried a child at five months gestation. They had been devastated by the loss. I remember his wife creating a photo album with ultrasound pictures of the baby. During his reading, my husband, Andrew, came through and said, "*Blood or not, this is still my grandchild.*"

Isabella told him that they would be having another child. They were saying, "No, no, no!" One night a few years later, I was lying in bed and got a call from my grandson. He was showing me a picture of their newborn.

I said, "Who is this?"

He said, "Your granddaughter."

I was completely surprised because I didn't even know they were expecting a child. They didn't know either!

Reda family siblings: Jesi (left), George, Angela (center); Joe (right).

They had gone to the hospital one night because of his wife's severe back pain. The nurses told her she was about to deliver! It turns out that she had even been menstruating all through the pregnancy. They were completely surprised. How can somebody go through a pregnancy and not know it? It beats me, but the proof is in the pudding. What Isabella predicted came true!

When Andrew passed away, I lost a lot of my faith. I asked myself, *How could this happen to someone like him? He was kind, loving, and never had a bad word to say about anyone.* And everybody who met him loved him. I was thinking, *Here are these horrible people out there who are alive and well, and Andrew, who is the greatest person in the world, and you take him?*

Now I realize that God doesn't take people. He lets them come to him. After talking with Isabella, my faith was restored. I thought, *That's where I want to go, to join my family members on the other side.*

I returned to reading my Bible and devotionals. My faith has greatly changed.

Andrew was a believer. He was raised as a Catholic and practiced all his life. When Isabella told me he was fine, I felt a sense of relief that I didn't have to worry about him being in Hell. It puts me at ease. He finished what he had to do here. Isabella confirmed it. She also told me many things about his brother, who passed before him, and described how the two make music together on the other side, playing the guitar. This is so comforting.

I'm just so grateful that I was able to talk with Isabella. This experience has completely changed my life, and I am now at peace.

RECONNECTING WITH OUR LOVED ONES OFTEN ABATES OUR SUFFERING

ISABELLA JOHNSON

The phrase "suffering is optional" has always brought such angst to me. We *do* suffer in life—we have physical pain, broken hearts, and a myriad of disappointments that can, at times, feel unsurpassable. It's hard enough when these challenges hit our lives, but it's nothing short of excruciating when they affect someone we love. Add to that a powerlessness to help or a less-than-perfect outcome for them, and grief can feel as if we are drowning.

Acceptance plays a huge part in this aspect of grief. Compare it to the first step in a recovery program—we truly are powerless to do anything but feel. Anger, which is merely sadness extended beyond ourselves, and depression, which is often sadness turned inward, are normal emotions and experiences during these times. Yes, we suffer.

Finding a path to reconnect with our loved ones often abates our suffering and gives us a breather to continue.

DEBBIE PRESCIANO

"Because I can connect directly with my son, I now have a purpose in life."

I have a husband and three living children. One of my children, a son, Jaime, is in Spirit. He crossed over when he was thirty-five. My son was diagnosed with Mesothelioma, a rare cancer, especially for those my son's age, because people usually get this type of cancer when in their sixties and seventies. It's so rare that hardly any doctors knew how to treat him. We were in shock. After extensive research, we found specialists who we hoped could treat him.

Jaime Presciano

We flew to see specialists in New York and Baltimore because it was such a rare cancer, and our hope laid with specialists in those cities. Jaime has always been extremely close with his siblings and they were there for him 24/7 during his illness, doing whatever he needed. My youngest son Nick, even quit his job at the time to be there for Jaime around the clock, making sure to give him his meds and the emotional support he needed. Most importantly, he brought Jaime's son, Carmen, to the hospital so he could see him. Carmen is his world. Unfortunately, the treatments didn't work, and he passed away in June 2019.

Presciano siblings Nick, Jaime, Kristi, and Tony

Before my experience of my child's transition, I didn't have a great deal of faith in the idea that people transitioned to the other side, much less about what they would be doing or be like there. I only believed in something that happened to me directly.

From the time he transitioned and for the next two years, I didn't do much of anything but exist. I was just going through the motions. When life's natural order of parents dying before their children is thrown out of order, it rearranges your world. During this time, I had had several readings with mediums, but nothing resonated with me. They didn't seem authentic.

Eventually, I joined Helping Parents Heal, and Isabella was among the mediums recommended. I decided to research Isabella and determine if I should contact her for a reading. After hearing some of the experiences others had had with Isabella, I decided to reach out. There was something genuine, just real, about her.

When I did have a reading with Isabella, I was blown away by the information she revealed to me. She mentioned many things she could have not possibly known before connecting with Jaime. I knew she was in touch with him.

The previous readings with others were nothing compared to Isbella's readings.

The validations and her presence left absolutely no doubt in the validity of Isabella and her readings.

Hands-on Dad

My son was a hands-on dad when he was here in the physical, and my grandson, Carmen, had just turned four when my son passed. He remembers his dad but not a whole lot about him. We play videos and show Jaime pictures of his dad on my phone.

Jaime and his son, Carmen Angelo

During a reading, Isabella mentioned that she saw a little boy approaching me at the same time my son came through. She estimated that he was between the ages of five and seven, which is how old my grandson is now. Jaime shared a lot about Carmen, that he watches over him, and how his son, Carmen, kisses his picture of my son, Jaime, every night. It was so validating when Isabella shared this detail. Jaime reiterated that he'd never leave him and would always watch over him.

Another example of how valid the readings are relates to my being executor of my son's will. Things didn't turn out as expected, and my son acknowledged this during a reading. Isabella described a white ranch house with a glass screen door on the front porch. She went on to say that it was currently empty and unoccupied but that I had a key to the house. Indeed, I had removed all the furniture, and it was empty because I was in the process of selling it. She had described my son's house. This information was so specific it simply blew me away.

Isabella mentioned that my son had smoked both cigarettes and medical marijuana when he was still here physically. He believed in medical marijuana, and it helped him manage some of the side effects of his cancer treatment, like chemo and radiation.

Jaime also told Isabella that I was suffering from depression, which I was. It's a family trait. My father had it, and I guess it was passed down. Even before my son's passing, I managed my depression with medication. During the reading, my son mentioned that he had also suffered from depression but had pushed it aside. This was astounding to me.

It's amazing how my son is still with me and that I can communicate with him. He hears and sees what's going on with me. I never would have believed it. Sometimes, I'll ask for signs. I talk to him. Sometimes I write letters to him.

During another reading with Isabella, I asked Jaime to send me a sign. She told me, "You are connected to him by dragonflies." I wondered about that. I'd never thought about dragonflies. Then, once, when I was sitting on the porch, a dragonfly flew under the overhang, stayed there for five minutes, and then flew away.

Another time, I went to the beach in Florida and saw a heart in the middle of the clouds. It stayed there for ten minutes and never moved!

A Life Dedicated to Family

Isabella could see the depth of my grief. She said it was so intense that it was even in my bones. Jaime told me, through Isabella, that he didn't want me to grieve anymore. He said, "I want you to live your life for me and Carmen." These words have helped me tremendously.

Because I can connect directly with Jaime, I now have a purpose in life.

Debbie and Jaime Presciano at Kristi's wedding in 2017.

PART TWO

EVOLVING MEDIUMSHIP

EVOLVING MEDIUMSHIP

ISABELLA JOHNSON

I had my first kid at nineteen. I just absolutely fell in love with being a mom and knew that was one of the things I was prepared to do. I had also known from early on that I would have a child that would die at a young age.

As a young mother and medium, I worked with clients for six to eight hours daily. This was before the Internet. One can imagine me holding a phone with a long chord that stretched all around the house.

I was a proficient medium at that time. When working with parents of children who had transitioned, I recognized that they were suffering from prolonged grief. Now, looking back, it feels like the evidence I was giving them was superficial or at least lacked emotion. I assured them that their children were still with them, yet I couldn't grasp the pain of that loss.

My Daughter's Lessons for Me

And then, I lost my child. When I lost my daughter, it was devastating. Yet, what a gift that was to become. I knew Collette was still with me, although it took some time to learn why she had died.

I remember needing firm answers from my guides, God, or anyone about why this happened. I wanted to know what I was supposed to do with my experience and what the gifts were. I was acutely depressed and situationally suicidal because of the pain. I didn't know how to deal with and make sense of that significant loss.

From the second when I woke up to the second when I went to bed, I grieved for about eighteen to nineteen months. In my case, I was supported by a support group for those who had lost a child, Compassionate Friends. At one of the meetings I attended, just three months after Collete transitioned, I met parents whose children had transitioned ten or fifteen years earlier and continued to be in a very dark place. I remember looking at my partner after that meeting and saying that I couldn't imagine feeling like I just wanted to die for the next ten or fifteen years or the rest of my life.

We didn't have answers for many years about why my daughter died. It turned out she had a genetic condition that she inherited from me. Her mitochondrial DNA is now being used to help other parents who have lost their children. On a soul level, I'm amazed by Collette's compassion and desire to be of service, even as a child.

One of the positive outcomes of losing my daughter was gaining a deeper understanding of the pain that family members feel when they lose a child. It allowed me to recognize and share a more profound knowledge with my clients who had suffered the loss of a child. As a result, I now always try to ease my client's pain and suffering however I can.

This experience of Collete's early departure put me on a very deep, intense, and profound spiritual journey, which again is another gift of her death.

The Beginning of My Healing

Finally, I began to connect with Collete and understand why she had left the physical plane and transitioned to the Spirit world. My readings with clients were changing. I was much more vulnerable and open to sharing my personal experience.

Understanding that Collette and I could never be separated was also a tremendous gift. This experience also propelled me to renegotiate my life and reevaluate everything. Nowadays, I don't see my child every day, but I know she's around. The same is true with my former husband, who is also in Spirit.

I asked myself: *Is what I'm doing actually what I want to be doing? Am I in the relationship that's feeding my soul?* I realized at that point my mortality became very front and center. I ended an unhealthy relationship. I now realize how immature I was and how immature my actions were then.

Honing My Mediumship Skills

After much meditation and soul-searching, I knew that I still had important things to do and would continue to fulfill my responsibilities based on my spiritual growth. As a result, in my late twenties and early thirties, I could muster the confidence to hone my mediumship skills. I had a good grasp of what it was like when we die and some of the reasons why we're here. I had been very naïve until this stage in my life and gradually began fulfilling my purpose.

One of my sons also has this ability and is comforted that this gift, which began with my grandmother, has been passed on to him.

As an aside, my children could never get away with lying to me. I always knew when they were telling the truth. Even today, they and their friends benefit from my ability to function as a conduit between them and their loved ones on the other side. Our whole family benefits from this gift of mediumship.

Those in Spirit Provide Information

Literally, before almost every reading, I get nervous and am always relieved when the spirits come in.

It's an honor to be a transactional part of my client's experience, even though I am humbled and slack-jawed at what transpires during our sessions. I'm proud of my work. I am a translator and a voice; honestly, I'd much rather be talking to the Spirits on the other side than you.

In the process, I do whatever the Spirits on the other side tell me. I work for them. I couldn't do anything I do if those in Spirit didn't allow me to merge with them and give them a voice. When we merge, all of their memories and experiences are known. They reveal everything that they recount and begin reliving everything. I can express this to the client.

I want to highlight that I don't make these people show up; I don't get them to talk. It cannot be overstated enough that the people in Spirit provide the information, not me, the medium. If other mediums don't feel that way, they are mistaken because it is evident that this has so little to do with the medium themselves.

The evidence comes from those in Spirit; it is the personality of the person in Spirit and the depth of the relationships on a nuanced level that can't be categorized with family members. None of the evidence can be located through Internet searches.

Very often, the person in Spirit discloses regrets and gives some explanation. This is usually very healing for the family members. And, very frequently, the family members tell the person in Spirit that they don't need to apologize. When the family members don't feel blamed or accused, they tend to blame themselves.

Professionalism: I Know Nothing About My Clients Before the Reading

I am not friends with my clients. My mediumship is a profound gift that has been verified many times over. For example, when participating in double or triple-blind tested scientific research groups of ten to twenty people over the years, I consistently landed at the top of the list, at number one or two.

I have always had someone to book clients for me, and I do that for a particular reason. The authenticity of my work is paramount. I didn't want any prior knowledge or information. I wanted the reading to be a cold read. I didn't want to know anything about the client before I met with them. I didn't want anything whatsoever to skew the reading.

Long ago, I stopped worrying about skeptics. I have clients of every faith and no faith. My favorite clients are atheists and agnostics. They are often astounded by the information they receive during the reading. In the end, at the very minimum, they often have hope. Hope can be fierce but can also get us through challenging moments. Hope can be intense, and it can also be something that gets us through difficult moments.

Family Therapist

I am a therapist. I work with families of those in Spirit and the family members who are still living. In most sessions, the person in Spirit initiates the discussion, and I speak for them. In other words, they are speaking through me. Most of my participation revolves around speaking on behalf of the person in Spirit.

Before meeting with every client, I always take a few minutes to pray, asking God to help me be of service to that person. I ask God for wisdom, knowledge, and understanding. I have a litany of those I ask for help—my guardians, guides, angels, ancestors, mothers, fathers, and God's council. I've continued to add people, deities, beings, and angels to that list as the years go on.

Then, as I become centered, I ask if anyone in Spirit wants to talk to my client. I will say the first name of the client and ask that my thoughts, memories, and emotions be replaced with the person in Spirit on the other side. I ask that the person in Spirit show up as they looked here in life the last lifetime so that their loved ones can recognize them.

I ask them to talk about their relationship and offer for the person in Spirit to tell me about themselves—their personality, what they love, and any areas or topics that need to be discussed. I ask if there are any signs my client has thought of that they'd want the person in Spirit to come through with and to make those very clear.

Then, I focus on the bottom of my stomach, hoping that when my client shows up a couple of minutes later, their loved ones will also.

I am somewhat anxious when I meet a client for the first time. I don't care if I've been doing this for a hundred years or over forty years; I know I am at the mercy of people in Spirit to show up.

I always have trust and confidence that the person in Spirit will be truthful. Any nervousness I may have felt is diminished once the person in Spirit appears. I laugh at myself because I'm over fifty, and it's only happened three times that no one has shown up. I believe the reason for that is the person seeking to speak to their loved one on the other side was intoxicated, and I think it blocked the possibility of communication with the person in Spirit.

With all of the people who come to greet their loved ones in the physical realm, they want to let their loved ones know that they're OK and that they're still with them.

I also ask if they can provide proof or evidence of what's going on with the client to let them know that they are still a part of their lives.

This seems to be very powerful for the client. Those in Spirit provide proof of who they are and show me about their personality. They often want to make amends or to own up to what they were doing while still alive. And I am sometimes surprised about those apologies because they sometimes seem mundane.

Clients love hearing from their loved ones in Spirit, no matter how trivial their concerns seem.

Usually, five to eight people in Spirit will appear at the beginning of a reading. The client usually has one or two people in mind that they want to talk to. I'll typically know immediately when I see the people in Spirit that the client wants to speak to. They tend to be outspoken, and I get a sense of who they are in relation to the client.

Often, the client is somewhat nervous or skeptical, and there is usually some anxiety on the client's part.

I try to reassure them, let them know what to expect, and then I begin with the reading. After that, I have to quickly identify the relationship of the person in Spirit with the client. I can physically describe them and learn about their personality. This happens within a matter of seconds. Sometimes the information is telepathic, sometimes visual, sometimes they're showing me in little movies. There is always emotion behind what the person in Spirit is saying or showing me. It is a full-sensory experience for me.

Imagine meeting eight new people in one hour and hearing about their life stories in such detail that you could write a book about them and then giving that information to someone else you don't know. I have to tie everything together, follow through with my intentions and attention in so many different places.

The communication happens so quickly that I assume that I am transforming in their energy because the recall is as if it's my memory.

A client might say they have a question, which is answered before it's even asked. Or they'll come in with five or six things they want to know, and every single one will be answered before I even say, "Do you have any questions?" The person in Spirit will answer everything. Often, the client will forget they are talking to Isabella and begin to have a conversation with Mom or Dad or their child. They might call the person by name, and I won't notice it. That's how effectively they can come through.

I see an average of eight to ten clients on a typical day. Along with the client, I'm seeing a minimum of five people in Spirit talking. Two or three of them speak in-depth and pass messages along. I don't ever worry about the people in Spirit. It's always the living that I have a concern about. I want to ensure the client leaves with their spirits lifted and encouraged. Rarely does someone not feel better after a reading. They leave knowing they are connected with their family, that their loved one is still around, that they are loved, that they have seen evidence of that, and that life goes on.

Questions are answered. Feelings are soothed. Wounds that weren't healed are healed with the people of Spirit. Very often, the result is closure for those in Spirit and family members. And then, the healing occurs. These discussions are heartfelt.

The clients in this family therapy and those on their other side experience tremendous closure. Some of these clients have profound, heavy, clinical grief. When communicating with those family members on the other side, they are unburdened, and the wounds are healed.

I do want to highlight this, and if it can be highlighted very adequately, I get a lot of credit for this, but that is wildly misplaced, in my opinion. I know I am the messenger and do a good job of passing along the message. However, these people show up ready to communicate. If a person in Spirit isn't prepared to communicate, I can usually encourage them to talk more and do all the heavy lifting.

I try to give my best, and I think it cannot be overstated enough that the people in Spirit and not the medium are making this happen.

My connection with Spirit has given me a different view on the seriousness of life. I say that, understanding the heaviness of that word. We are supposed to have fun here and find joy and happiness, but this is where we learn profound lessons for ourselves and others. I've learned that when we slack off in any way, we often know we didn't do our best, and there is a regret.

Having learned this from people on the other side, I am taking my relationships with people much more seriously than I did before. Being present and listening is essential, so I am much more mindful of the people I want to interact with personally. I know how meaningful those relationships are to my spiritual growth.

ABOUT ISABELLA JOHNSON

Isabella Johnson continues her over four decades-long practice of working with clients worldwide. She considers her mediumship is a gift that has been verified many times over on a scientific and academic basis, including certification as an Evidential Certified Medium by Mark Ireland, co-founder of the non-profit organization, Helping Parents Heal. As a grief recovery specialist, remote viewer, and counselor, Isabella has committed her life to providing comfort, healing and hope to the bereaved. Isabella firmly believes that each of our souls survives the transition called death, and endeavors to bring evidence that those in Spirit are always with us.

www.ingramcontent.com/pod-product-compliance
Lightning Source LLC
LaVergne TN
LVHW022116200926
848481LV00003B/1176